Southern Rails
On Southampton
Docks
Including the Industrial Lines
of Southampton

Ian Drummond

For
Peter Clark

Holne Publishing

© Holne Publishing & Ian Drummond 2013
British Library Cataloguing in Publication Data
A record for this book is available from the British Library
ISBN 978-0-9563317-4-8
Published by: Holne Publishing, PO Box 343, LEEDS, LS19 9FW
Typesetting and Photo Restoration by: Holne Publishing Services, PO Box 343, LEEDS, LS19 9FW
Printed by: Charlesworth Press, Flanshaw Way, Flanshaw Lane, Wakefield, WF2 9LP

Reasonable efforts have been made to discover the true copyright owners of the photographs reproduced in this volume, and no infringement of copyright is intended. If you have any evidence about the copyright owner of any photograph, or the photographer of any photograph listed as 'photographer unknown', please contact the publisher in the first instance. Uncredited photographs are by the author.

Photographs in this volume have been digitally adjusted to enhance clarity, and also remove blemishes, dust etc. However, no intentional alterations have been made to affect their historical significance.

Unless otherwise indicated all maps are based on Ordnance Survey maps of the appropriate date, and their top edge represents north. Maps are reproduced to no particular scale other than where indicated.

Holne Publishing
PO Box 343
LEEDS
LS19 9FW
enquiries@holnepublishing.co.uk
www.holnepublishing.co.uk

Cover Photos:

Front:
Top: *Lord Nelson* class No.30857 *Lord Howe* prepares to depart from Ocean Terminal with *The Cunarder* in 1956.
(Photo: P.B. Whitehouse Copyright Colour-Rail BRS995)
Bottom: *USA* class No.30067 at work near Ocean Terminal with the sun setting in 1958.
(Photo: A.C. Sterndale Copyright Colour-Rail BRS1276)

Back: On 12th July 1970 class 07s Nos.2987 and 2996 are seen in the Eastern Docks. No.2996 still survives at Scunthorpe Steelworks.
(Photo: Gordon Edgar Copyright RailPhotoprints)

Contents

Map of Southampton Showing The Old and New Docks, Main Line and Principal Industrial Railways

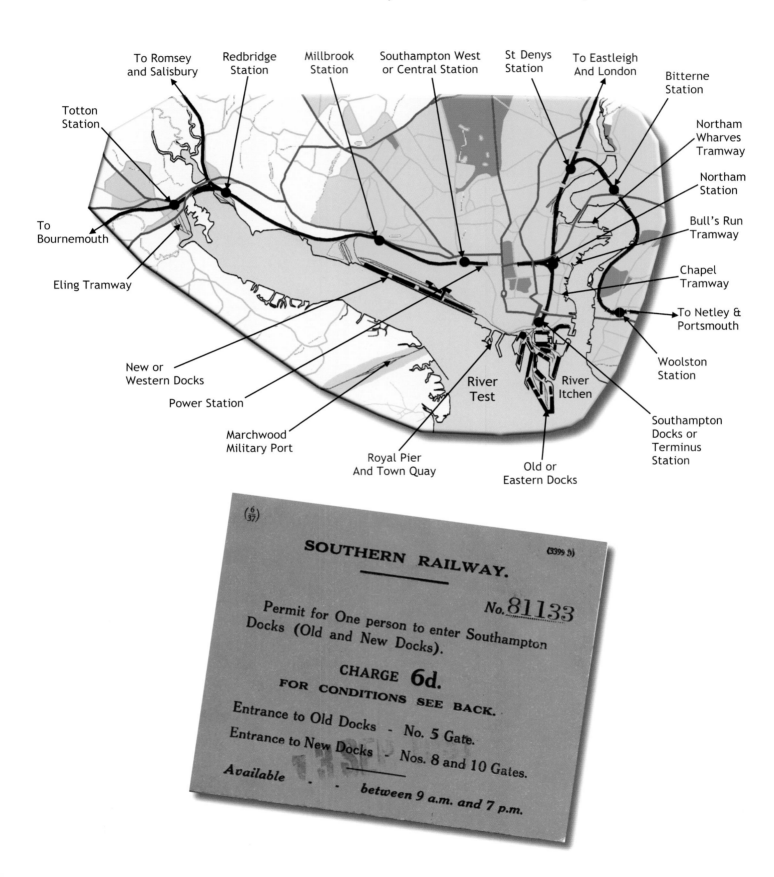

To Romsey and Salisbury

Redbridge Station

Millbrook Station

Southampton West or Central Station

St Denys Station

To Eastleigh And London

Bitterne Station

Totton Station

Northam Wharves Tramway

Northam Station

To Bournemouth

Bull's Run Tramway

Eling Tramway

Chapel Tramway

To Netley & Portsmouth

New or Western Docks

Woolston Station

Power Station

River Test

River Itchen

Southampton Docks or Terminus Station

Marchwood Military Port

Royal Pier And Town Quay

Old or Eastern Docks

$\left(\frac{6}{37}\right)$

(3399 3)

SOUTHERN RAILWAY.

No. 81133

Permit for One person to enter Southampton Docks (Old and New Docks).

CHARGE 6d.

FOR CONDITIONS SEE BACK.

Entrance to Old Docks - No. 5 Gate.

Entrance to New Docks - Nos. 8 and 10 Gates.

Available between 9 a.m. and 7 p.m.

Foreword

Above: BR standard class 5 No.73155 stands outside the photographer's open office window (top left) waiting to be allowed across the Canute Road crossing in April 1967.

(Photo: T. Hastings)

At their height the railways of Southampton Docks extended to a total of 77 miles. This was longer than the main line from Southampton to Waterloo, with nearly 1,000 hand-operated points. In addition, there were no signals except at the crossing across Canute Road. However, in some ways they were a closed world behind walls and gates with access only by permission.

But without the railways the docks could not have functioned and grown to the extent that they did, such that the Port of Southampton could proclaim itself to be the *Gateway to the World*. There was, and indeed still is, a symbiotic relationship between the town, docks and railways to the mutual benefit of all. Of course during the nineteenth and early twentieth century the Empire was also significant, as it was the major source of trade, with many of the imports and exports through the ports either originating in, or being shipped to the colonies.

When originally planning *Southern Rails Around Southampton* my intention was to include the docks railways as simply one chapter within the book. However, as research progressed it became clear that there was much more to the story of the railways of the docks and indeed the other industrial lines in and around Southampton than could be contained in just a few pages. Therefore, the decision was made to make this a separate volume, readers of *Southern Rails Around Southampton*

will appreciate that this did not leave us short of material for that book!

This led to more research resulting in this volume, which in many ways has been a very different book to write compared to the previous books in this series. Much time has been spent at record offices and reading minute books trying to piece together the story of the docks railways, and their operation. However, I do not claim that this is anything like their definitive history.

Of course, as ever, it is right to acknowledge those who have produced earlier works, Bert Moody once again provided invaluable assistance. In addition, Dave Marden's two books on Southampton's quayside railways have also proved an excellent source of information, and are recommended reading for those wanting to know more, particularly about the many locomotives that were employed.

From this history emerges a story that is really the tale of two docks. The first, now known as the Eastern Docks, grew in an organic, piecemeal, way over about seventy years. New quays and facilities were added as traffic grew and the size of ships increased, while the railways that served the berths grew in a similar fashion. This resulted in a layout that was in its heyday quite chaotic in places, with tight curves, and lines criss-crossing one another. In

Above: Southampton Town Quay with class C14 locomotive No.30589, built in 1907 as a 2-2-0T and rebuilt in 1923 as an 0-4-0T, shunting on the quayside in August 1952. The *Murius* in the foreground was built in 1888, and was one of a number of barges that carried freight to the Isle of Wight from Southampton. However, *Murius* also took part in Operation Dynamo during World War Two as one of the 'little ships' that rescued troops from the beaches of Dunkirk.   (Photo: S.C.Townroe Copyright Colour-Rail BRS795)

turn this placed restrictions on the types of locomotives that could be used there.

By contrast the New, or Western, Docks as they are now known, and their railways were the epitome of an efficiently planned system. It has to be said that the reclamation of over 400 acres of land would probably not have been allowed today, completely changing the shoreline on the south-west side of the town as it did. Nevertheless it enabled the design of a railway system with ease of access to all facilities, as well the provision of more than adequate marshalling yards and other essentials.

Both these docks were different, and both have served the port, town and nation well, especially during the dark days of war. This was particularly true in the run-up to and aftermath of D-Day. Hopefully through this book how the railways enabled the docks to fulfil their role will become clearer, and will encourage others to develop further work on this fascinating aspect of the economic and social history of the now City of Southampton.

Coupled with the docks lines we must not forget the other industrial lines of the city. The former Harbour Board lines are perhaps the most well known, as they were where the docks trains could be seen 'in public', serving the Town Quay for many years, and latterly providing part of the link between the two docks.

Then there were the privately owned lines at Northam

Wharves, the Chapel and Eling Tramways, and the Power Station line. However, perhaps the most well-known of these was the line originally known as 'Bull's Run' or latterly the Dibles Wharf line. This was home to what was to be the last working steam locomotive in the city, the ex-docks tank locomotive that became known as *Corrall Queen*, now happily preserved at the Bluebell Railway. All these lines are now only memories, but again hopefully this volume will add what is known of their history.

As ever there are so many people to thank, and I am bound to miss someone out, but I would particularly mention Terry Hastings and Roger Silsbury, for providing photos from behind the walls. In addition, there are those who offered support when they heard this book was being written. I would especially mention Russell Burridge who volunteered images of artefacts from his late father Frank's collection. High on the list too must come the staff at the Southampton Record Office for all their help.

There is also my regular team of helpers, my wife Di, Dr Alan Doe, Lawrie Bowles, and John and Barbara Plumtree-Varley. This book is dedicated to my father-in-law Peter Clark; he like many others passed through Southampton on their way to their National Service postings, so perhaps they might not view the port in the most favourable of lights, except when they were coming home. However, without Peter's generous support Holne Publishing would not exist and it is a pleasure to be able to say thank you in a public way on behalf of those who have enjoyed our previous books, and, I hope, will enjoy this one.

A Brief History of Southampton Docks

As was seen in the companion book to this volume *Southern Rails Around Southampton*, Southampton had functioned as a port for centuries, being for many years the principal port for Winchester. Its geographical position, as a sheltered harbour at the head of Southampton Water, and the shape of the Solent, which produces the famous 'double' high tide, means that Southampton enjoys many natural advantages as a port. However, it was not until the early nineteenth century that the developments began that would turn the town into the major maritime city it is today.

Above: The Borough Arms of Southampton.

The Harbour Commissioners

In 1803 an Act was passed leading to the establishment of the Harbour Commissioners, who were to have responsibility for the dredging and maintenance of the waters around Southampton, as well as overseeing the then existing port facilities outside the Water Gate. From here Henry V had set sail for Agincourt, and the Pilgrim Fathers had sailed for the New World.

Quickly they set about developing a new quay, known as Town Quay, and in 1818 sailing ships began a regular service from there to Le Havre in addition to the well established services to the Isle of Wight, Channel Islands and other destinations. Paddle steamers first plied the route to the Isle of Wight on 24th June 1820 and subsequently steamers were used on both the Channel Islands and Le Havre routes. Then in 1833 the Royal Victoria Pier, later known simply as the Royal Pier, was opened. Originally a wooden structure it was subsequently replaced with one constructed of cast iron.

The Establishment of the Docks

It was also around this time that moves began to establish deep water docks at the port, not by the Harbour Commissioners due to the financial limits imposed on them by statute, but instead by those promoting the new railway to London. Originally the new docks were to be an integral part of the proposed railway, and it was planned to seek Parliamentary authority for both as one undertaking named the Southampton, London and Branch Railway and Dock Company. However, it was soon decided to separate the two enterprises. Therefore, the Southampton Docks Company (SDC) was authorised by Act of Parliament in May 1836 with a capital of £350,000.

On 12th October 1838 the foundation stone was laid initiating work on the first stage of the docks on 216 acres of mudlands the company had purchased for £5,000. This was to be a tidal basin, later known as the Outer Dock, covering an area of 16 acres with 2,600ft of quays. The

Right: The opening of the enlarged entrance to the Inner Dock on 20th May 1859 with the P&O steamship *Pera* entering the Dock.
(From *The Illustrated London News*)

new dock was opened on 29th August 1842 along with a rail link to the now-named London and South Western Railway (LSWR) at Southampton station, which had opened through to London in 1840.

Further Developments

Quickly further developments followed, three dry docks were completed between 1846 and 1854, while on 4th December 1851 the Inner Dock was opened. This was a ten acre non-tidal basin built west of the Outer Dock some 804ft by 550ft, constructed at a cost of £23,000.

These new developments came as a result of the rapid expansion in the number of ships using the port, these included those of the Peninsular and Orient Line (P&O), and the Royal Mail Steam Packet Company. In addition, there were also ships of the New South Western Steam Packet Company established by the LSWR, and taken over by them in 1862. The first transatlantic steam services were operated by the Ocean Steam Navigation Company in 1847. Such new services, along with other traffic, contributed to the prosperity of the Dock Company, which in January 1846 was able to lend £10,000 to the LSWR to help them fund further developments.

In 1873 work was started on the Itchen Quays with berths 30 to 33 completed in 1876, while another dry dock (No.4) was opened in 1879. Then in 1886 the Dock Company began its most ambitious project, the 18.5 acre Empress Dock. By this time fortunes had changed, particularly after P&O moved its base of operations to London in 1875. Therefore, to fund the work the SDC took out a £250,000 loan from the LSWR. Work on the new dock was completed in 1890 and it was opened by Queen Victoria on 26th July that year.

Takeover by the LSWR

However, the SDC was still suffering from a cash shortage to develop further facilities for the larger ships then coming into service, and so in March 1891 they approached the LSWR with a view to the latter taking over the docks. Agreement was eventually reached for the LSWR to purchase the docks at a cost of £1.36 million, which was approved by the SDC directors in December 1891 and the LSWR assumed control in 1892.

The LSWR immediately set about further developments, constructing berths 34 to 36 on the River Itchen, which were completed in 1895. In addition, the Prince of Wales (No.5) Dry Dock was opened the same year. Meanwhile, in 1894 Southampton had been made the principal port for peacetime troop movements, a role it was to play until 1962. Further work saw the completion of South Quay (berth 37) and the Test Quays (berths 38 to 41) in 1902, berth 40 being the site of the International Cold Store.

Ships were still getting larger, which necessitated an even larger dry dock. Therefore, the Trafalgar Dry Dock was opened on 21st October 1905. Then when the White Star Line proposed transferring its North Atlantic liners to the port from Liverpool a new 15.5 acre dock was built. This was completed in 1911 and named the White Star Dock, but was renamed Ocean Dock in 1922. It was from this dock that the *Titanic* set out on its ill-fated maiden voyage on 10th April 1912.

Elsewhere the Trafalgar Dry Dock reopened in 1911 having been enlarged. This was in preference to a proposal to build a new dock on the Woolston side of the river Itchen, referred to on page 132 of *Southern Rails Around Southampton*. At this point what were to become known as the Old, or Eastern Docks were more or less complete. Later developments would come after the takeover of the docks by the Southern Railway (SR).

World War One

Southampton's status as the prime trooping port meant that in times of conflict it could be a busy place. Even

Right: The Royal Mail Steam Packet Co's 'A' class liner *Almanzora* in the Empress Dock. On the left the cargo is being hand-loaded into the waiting covered vans. The crane is probably hydraulically operated, and of an elegant design. The *Almanzora* was completed in 1915, seeing service first as an armed cruiser during World War One. After the war it was employed on the route to Brazil, Uruguay and Argentina, and was able to carry nearly 1,400 passengers. It was used as a troopship during World War Two and laid up in 1947 before being scrapped the following year.
(Commercial Postcard)

Above: Three of the fourteen four-funnelled liners ever built berthed in Ocean Dock. On the left at berth 43 is the *Olympic*, sister ship to the *Titanic* owned by the White Star Line, launched in 1911. At berth 47 in the centre is the *Aquitania*, launched in 1913 and owned by Cunard, while on the right at berth 46 is the *Mauretania* launched in 1906. This photo was probably taken around 1920. (Commercial Postcard)

before it had been given its official status it had still been used for troop embarkation, playing a significant role in both the Crimean and Boer wars.

However, the First World War saw all normal traffic through the port suspended, apart from a limited cross-channel ferry operation, as Southampton became the Number One Embarkation Port. One particular type of traffic was casualties being returned from the front for treatment at the Royal Victoria Hospital at Netley, which will be detailed later. This was allied with the provision of a train ferry service, which used a purpose-built jetty west of the Royal Pier between 1917 and 1919.

Grouping and the New Docks

After the war it was realised that substantial new facilities were required at the port, particularly in view of the still increasing size of ships. Therefore, the LSWR began to consider new options. In 1922 a scheme was announced for the reclamation of 648 acres of mudland behind a two mile long bank between the Royal Pier and Millbrook Point. From this five jetties would be built each 1,000ft long, as well as two graving docks, with rail access provided by a triangular junction with the main line between Millbrook and Redbridge.

But before these plans could move forward the LSWR became part of the SR. However, it did place an order in October 1922 for a 960ft long and 134ft wide floating dry dock at a cost of £375,000. This was officially inaugurated on 27th June 1924, being berthed between the docks and Town Quay.

Between 1892 and 1922, the period the LSWR had owned the docks, traffic had increased from 421,600 tons of cargo being handled annually to 742,834 tons. During the same period passenger numbers also rose from 122,000 to 356,110 annually.

The SR also recognised the need for new facilities. In October 1925 the first stage of a new development was proposed west of Royal Pier involving the construction of two jetties with four berths each, along the lines of the previous LSWR plan, with a rail connection from Southampton West. However by July 1926 this had changed to a phased development involving the construction of a continuous quay wall from the Royal Pier to Millbrook Point, some 7,400ft long, with 407 acres of mudland reclaimed behind it. There would be a rail connection at Millbrook where two graving docks would be constructed. In addition there was a plan to build a 5000ft long jetty parallel with the quay wall (see plan on page 12). At the Royal Pier end a new rail connection would be made with the Harbour Board's line to Town Quay, and a new 400ft quay wall constructed between Town Quay and Royal Pier. This project was to be built in three stages, but in the end the third, including the jetty, was never completed.

Construction started on the first phase in 1927, with an estimated cost of £3 million. This was after the completion of various pieces of land purchase, including the old train ferry terminal and jetty, which was purchased from the government for £3,500. In addition, 116 acres of mudland was obtained from Southampton Corporation, the majority of which was handed back

Development of the Old Docks

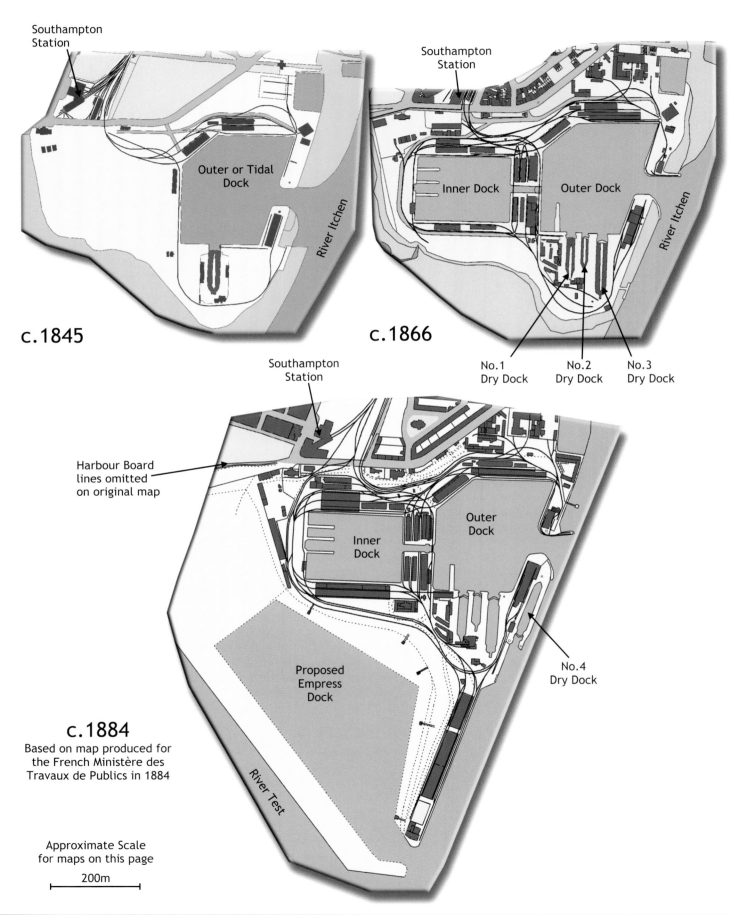

Southampton Station

Outer or Tidal Dock

River Itchen

c.1845

Southampton Station

Inner Dock

Outer Dock

River Itchen

c.1866

No.1 Dry Dock

No.2 Dry Dock

No.3 Dry Dock

Southampton Station

Harbour Board lines omitted on original map

Outer Dock

Inner Dock

No.4 Dry Dock

Proposed Empress Dock

c.1884

Based on map produced for the French Ministère des Travaux de Publics in 1884

River Test

Approximate Scale for maps on this page

200m

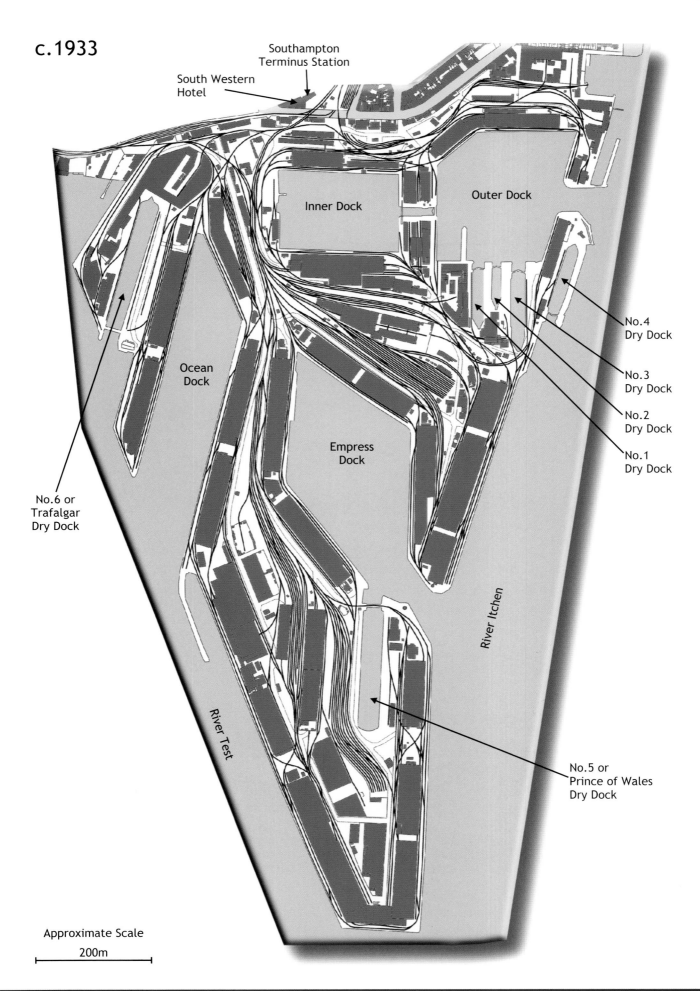

c.1933

Southampton
Terminus Station

South Western
Hotel

Inner Dock

Outer Dock

Ocean
Dock

No.4
Dry Dock

No.3
Dry Dock

No.2
Dry Dock

No.1
Dry Dock

Empress
Dock

No.6 or
Trafalgar
Dry Dock

River Itchen

River Test

No.5 or
Prince of Wales
Dry Dock

Approximate Scale

200m

Plan of Proposed New Docks Including Parts Not Built
(Based on Southern Railway Plan)

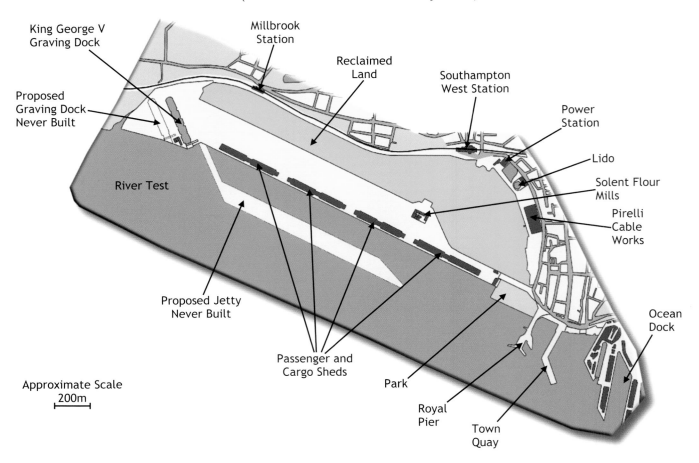

King George V Graving Dock

Millbrook Station

Reclaimed Land

Southampton West Station

Power Station

Lido

Solent Flour Mills

Pirelli Cable Works

Proposed Graving Dock Never Built

River Test

Proposed Jetty Never Built

Passenger and Cargo Sheds

Park

Royal Pier

Town Quay

Ocean Dock

Approximate Scale 200m

Left: The *Queen Mary* entering the King George V graving dock, with the New Docks in the background, showing the vast expanse of reclaimed land yet to be occupied. The pool of water nearest the camera beside the graving dock was left un-reclaimed because this was going to be the site of a second graving dock, which in the end was not built.

(Photo: Southern Railway Courtesy BRB)

when work was completed, with ten acres becoming Mayflower Park. Other land was purchased from the Barker Mill family at a cost of £45,000 after arbitration.

By November 1930 the first stage of the new extensions were well under way and the second stage was approved, which considering the economic conditions of the time following the Wall Street Crash, was a brave decision. On 19th October 1932 the *Mauretania* berthed at the first of the new quays, and the first stage of the docks extension was nearly complete. On 26th July 1933 the new graving dock was opened by King George V, and was named after him. This was first used by the *Majestic* on 19th January 1934. Eventually eight new berths were provided along the new quay wall (nos. 101 to 108), but the second graving dock and jetty never materialised.

Developments in the Old Docks

While much attention was on the New Docks extension there were also developments in the Old Docks. New sheds were provided at various locations, while 'K' warehouse, north of the Inner Dock, which had burnt down in a fire in 1925 was replaced by a distribution centre for Cadburys in 1928. To help with the movement of goods around the docks electric trucks were acquired during the 1920s, with 48 in service by 1928. In addition extra timber storage sheds were built by berth 45 in the Ocean Dock, with a floor area of 72,000 sq ft.

During the 1930s trading was difficult with the effects of the Great Depression, cargo tonnage handled at the docks fell from just under 1.2 million tons in 1927 to 0.86 million tons in 1932. Similarly passenger numbers fell from 481,362 to 473,578 over the same period. However, by 1937 trade had improved. Over that year nearly 1.3 million tons of cargo passed through the port, along with 622,000 passengers. This was nearly 50% of the United Kingdom's ocean-going passenger traffic making Southampton the United Kingdom's *Premier Passenger Port*.

This was very much the age of the great transatlantic liners, with names such as the *Mauretania, Leviathan, Britannic, Empress of Britain,* and of course the *Queen Mary*. The *Queen Elizabeth*, it should be noted, never entered peacetime service before the war. However, the late 1930s saw the development of Imperial Airways Flying Boat service which operated from Southampton. But all this was to change with the outbreak of World War Two.

World War Two

At the start of the war the port was closed to all but coastal shipping. This enabled it to be used for the embarkation of troops to the continent in 1939. However, Southampton also played a role in the evacuation from Dunkirk, and was also a haven for boats bringing refugees from France, Holland and Belgium. Hundreds of small

Above: First the LSWR and later the SR purchased battery-electric trolleys for moving goods around the docks. Although not brought as replacements for shunting locomotives they were, as here, used for shunting within the docks.
(Photo: Southampton Record Office/Associated British Ports)

craft were berthed at the docks, sometimes a dozen abreast. In addition many French troops evacuated at Dunkirk were returned to their own country through the port.

The port was also subject to many bombing raids. In August 1940 the cold store at berth 40 received a direct hit. The fire brigade, which turned out while the bombs were still falling, was hampered by the fact that the mains water supply had also been hit. Then in November 1940, there was a particularly heavy series of attacks, which severely damaged parts of the docks.

On the night of 23rd November over 40 bombs fell on the Old and New Docks destroying the Canadian Pacific Offices, while the Docks Central Fire Station and its fire engine also took a direct hit. A week later there was an even heavier raid at the docks when two warehouses were destroyed. In addition the Harland & Wolff works, along with the Rank Flour Mills and General Motors Factory, were badly damaged.

Later raids, although not as severe, also caused damage, and the Docks Fire Brigade, of which the author's father was a member between 1941 and 1946, was called upon to deal with a wide variety of incidents including fires on ships damaged in attacks on convoys. In total during World War Two there were 69 air raids, which resulted in the destruction of 23 warehouses or transit sheds.

In 1942 the docks had been reopened for 'lease-lend' traffic from the United States, often conveyed on *Liberty* ships. Meanwhile a new heavily bunkered control centre was constructed in the Old Docks.

Of course the greatest challenge for the docks came with the build-up to D-Day. As part of the preparations new equipment and cranes, along with new rail sidings and

other pieces of infrastructure were provided. A train ferry terminal was established near the King George V Dock, and all over the port and surrounding area additional berthing and embarkation points were created. Meanwhile many of the dry docks, and some of the berthing capacity, were given over to the construction and 'stock piling' of components for the 'Mulberry' harbours used in the D-Day landings.

A special executive committee was also established to oversee operations through the port. That all this was done in secrecy is amazing; part of this was achieved by creating an artificial 'fog' over the town, shrouding the preparations from aerial observation. Even a visit by Winston Churchill to the docks on 3rd June, three days before the ships sailed on 6th June 1944, failed to alert many to the imminent departure of forces.

Following D-Day, troop reinforcements were sent to Europe, while traffic also began to flow in the other direction. Casualties were returned, and German POWs were brought to Britain. Ships also returned damaged and in need of urgent repair. It is estimated that in the seventeen weeks following D-Day the port handled more goods than for the whole of 1938.

Nationalisation

Following the war there were plans to replace what was lost during the conflict, and to provide new facilities. Part of the SR's plans were for two six-storey warehouses 400ft long and 100ft wide. The first of these was planned for the western end of the New Docks estate, but was never constructed.

Other plans which did proceed were for a new cold storage building alongside berth 108, and a new maritime terminal at berth 50 for British Overseas Airways

Left: In the midst of the devastation caused by the bombing a new reinforced control centre is built just to the north of the Inner Dock. Above it to the left are the remains of the sheds at berth 12. In the background a ship is berthed in Ocean Dock, and to the right are the Harland and Wolff works.
(Photo: Southampton Record Office/Associated British Ports)

Corporation's (BOAC) flying boat services. Additional land was also purchased in 1946 for proposed further extensions of the docks between Millbrook and Redbridge. The same year plans were drawn up for the building of a new terminal building at Ocean Dock. This would be known as Ocean Terminal. However, before most of these plans could be completed the docks were nationalised, coming under the jurisdiction of the British Transport Commission on 1st January 1948. Subsequently they became part of the Docks and Inland Waterways Executive from 1st January 1950 and then the British Transport Docks division from 1953.

The 1950s

The new Marine Air Terminal for BOAC opened on 14th April 1948. This consisted of a two-storey L-shaped building, with a direct rail connection through the docks to London. Meanwhile Ocean Terminal opened on 31st July 1950, at 1,270ft long with very distinctive architecture, it became a symbol of the port in the 1950s and 1960s handling most of the transatlantic liner traffic.

There were other developments during the 1950s including the opening of a new building at 102 berth for Union Castle Line's South African service in 1956, and the aforementioned cold store, which opened in 1958. New

passenger accommodation was also completed at berths 105/6 in November 1960.

A Time of Change

It was to be the 1960s that would herald the start of many changes for the port. During the mid to late 1950s the rise in air travel began to have an impact on the transatlantic passenger traffic. Other changes were also taking place. In 1961 British Railways switched its Channel Islands ferry service to Weymouth, and later in 1964 the Le Havre and St Malo services ceased, although the cargo service to the Channel Islands remained until 1972. However new car ferry operators came to start services both to familiar and new destinations.

While transatlantic numbers were in decline there was a rise in the demand for cruises and so two new passenger terminals were opened, the Mayflower terminal at berth 106 in 1960, and the Queen Elizabeth II terminal at 38/39 berth in 1966. 1969 saw the maiden voyage of the last great transatlantic liner, the *Queen Elizabeth 2 (QE2)*, built at John Brown's shipyard on the Clyde and launched in 1967. However, even the *QE2* had been designed for cruising during the winter as there was not enough traffic to justify a year round transatlantic service.

Above: Ocean Terminal nearing completion on 15th June 1950. The platform running the length of the outside of the building can clearly be seen, while the *USA* class locomotive in the foreground appears to still be in SR livery.

(Photo: Bert Moody Collection Courtesy BRB)

Similarly a major change was about to take place in the nature of the freight traffic passing through the port, this was due to the rise of the freight container. The history of containerisation at Southampton will be dealt with later, but in 1965 plans were announced for a £60 million extension to the Western Docks in order to build berths to handle the new container ships. They were built on the land between Millbrook and Redbridge acquired by the SR in 1946. Berth 201 came into use in October 1968, by which time the Freightliner rail terminal at Millbrook was also open, and later additions followed.

Moving into the 1970s further new container berths numbered 202 to 204 opened in 1972, and by May 1978 berths 205 and 206 were in use. The Maritime Container rail terminal had also been opened in 1972, so containers could be easily transferred from ship to rail. However, the 70s also saw further decline in regular passenger sailings with the ending of the Union Castle South African service in 1977. By this time the Inner Dock had been closed (in 1963) and was later filled in. The No.5 (Prince of Wales) Dry Dock was also closed and filled in 1977. The Eastern Docks (as they were known from 1964) were beginning to be run down.

Privatisation

In 1982 the British Transport Docks Board, which had come into existence in 1963 and had absorbed the Harbour Board in 1968, was privatised as Associated British Ports. That same year Southampton became a troop embarkation port once again as the 'Task Force' was assembled to go to the Falklands, which included the requisitioned cruise liners *QE2* and *Canberra*.

However, in and around the docks themselves other developments were taking place. The area around the old Outer Dock, renamed the Princess Alexandra Dock, was redeveloped as Ocean Village, which also included the site of the old Inner Docks. Town Quay was also redeveloped. Ocean Terminal was out of use by December 1980, and was demolished in 1983 after a life of just over thirty years. Another loss to the port was the transfer of the cross-channel ferries to Portsmouth in 1983 & 1984. There were, though, new facilities built for the handling of various types of freight in Eastern and Western Docks. As a result the freight tonnage handled through the port continued to grow.

Through the 90s and into the 21st Century

The development of facilities has continued through the 1990s. In 1996 berth 207 was brought into use and other facilities developed at the container port, as well as in the older parts of the docks. With the continuing surge in cruising two new cruise terminals were opened; City Terminal at berth 101 in 2003 and a new Ocean Terminal at berth 46 in 2009. Plans have even been mooted for a fifth terminal. A significant trade in recent years has also been the import and export of cars, and facilities built on various parts of the estate support this.

In the late 1990s Associated British Ports forwarded plans for a new container terminal on the opposite side of the river Test on Dibden Bay. However, a subsequent public inquiry resulted in the application being turned down on environmental grounds. Meanwhile further development of the container port has taken place and consideration is again being given to a revival of the Dibden Bay scheme possibly based around Marchwood Military Port.

Left: The former Outer Dock, now known as the Princess Alexandra Dock, has been redeveloped as part of Southampton's Ocean Village, and now serves as a marina.

The Development of the Docks Railways

Early Days

A rail connection was in place between the LSWR station in Southampton and the Outer Dock by the time that the latter opened on 29th August 1842. This seems to have been a simple affair laid between the station and the north-west corner of the dock, so that railway wagons could be moved across Canute Road into the docks for the transfer of goods. However, shortly after the opening a new connecting line was laid from Canute Road to the north-west quay warehouse, with a second line splitting off and looping to the eastern end of the north-west quay, where it connected to the warehouse lines by means of two wagon turntables.

This system was then extended along the north quay, and the east quay, with connections to a timber yard. After this connections were made to the south and south-east quays to the extent that by the end of 1844 it was stated that the rail system around the dock was completed. However, the completion of the first dry dock on the south side of the basin led to the line being diverted around the dry dock in a loop (see plan overleaf).

Initially the docks line seems to have been worked by horses. However, an interesting note in the SDC minutes in September 1844 stated that an agreement had been reached with the LSWR for the conveyance of goods from London to the docks. This included the clause that the LSWR were to be permitted to work their locomotives to a 'safe point within the docks as determined by the principal engineer of the LSWR'. The agreement was for an initial period of twelve months, and does not seem to have been rescinded. Horses would, though, continue to work wagons in the docks for many years.

Unwanted Advances

By mid-1847 several possible incursions into the docks by other lines had been fought off. First of all was a proposal by the Southampton and Dorchester Railway (S&DR) in 1844 to loop their line through the docks area to make a connection with the LSWR station, as well as to provide access to the docks. This was rejected by the SDC, and the S&DR eventually linked with the LSWR by an inland route. In 1846 it was the Manchester and Southampton Railway (M&SR), which proposed a line into the docks, or up to the docks boundary with free access into the docks. Initially the SDC opposed the scheme, but later, doubtless in line with the agreement the LSWR reached with the M&SR, they supported the line. However, in the end it was not built.

Another possible incursion came from closer to home with a proposal from the Harbour Commissioners in 1847. This was to build a tramway linking the Town Quay to the LSWR station via the docks premises. The tramway will be dealt with in a later chapter, but suffice to say the SDC was not happy with the idea which they opposed vigorously.

Above: The earliest illustration of railway operations at the docks, from 1852, shows the first line in place on the north quay of the Inner Dock. The wagon has been hand-loaded, and is shown being hand-shunted, possibly just up to the warehouse.

(From the *Illustrated London News*)

c.1845

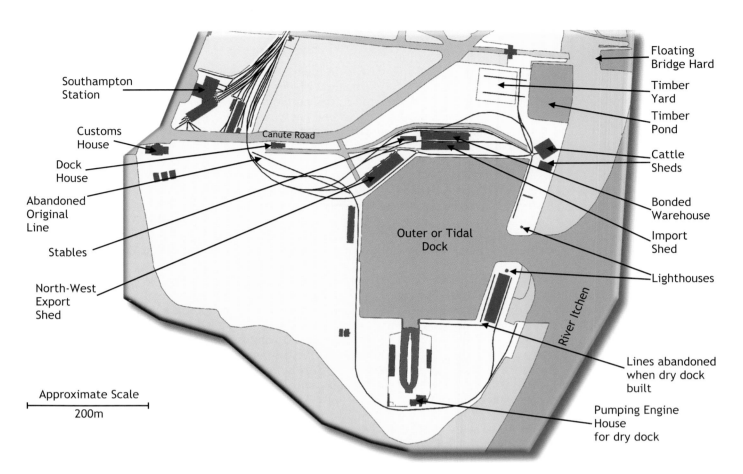

Southampton Station

Customs House

Dock House

Abandoned Original Line

Stables

North-West Export Shed

Canute Road

Outer or Tidal Dock

River Itchen

Floating Bridge Hard

Timber Yard

Timber Pond

Cattle Sheds

Bonded Warehouse

Import Shed

Lighthouses

Lines abandoned when dry dock built

Pumping Engine House for dry dock

Approximate Scale
200m

Further Developments

Meanwhile the docks continued to be developed. A second dry dock was added in 1847 which led to a rearrangement to the lines there. The amount of traffic carried meant that the original line along the north-east quay of the Outer Dock required renewal in 1848. Further lines also needed to be renewed the following year.

When the Inner Dock was opened in December 1851 a line was already in place along the north quay. Later forty tons of rails were purchased, so that lines could be laid along the western and southern quays of the dock in September 1852. By this time a new line from the terminus station was laid to replace the previous connection, which was truncated at the turntable for the Town Quay tramway.

In March 1852 Queen Victoria first made use of the docks when she returned from Osborne House. *The Standard* reported that a twelve carriage train was shunted to the north-west corner of the Outer Dock for the Queen to use. An LSWR locomotive was employed as motive power, with LSWR Locomotive Superintendent, Mr J. Beattie, supervising the driving and Mr Stovin, General Manager of the LSWR, acting as guard.

Relations with the LSWR

There were close links between the LSWR and the SDC,

indeed it was very much a symbiotic relationship. This is demonstrated by the fact that the LSWR had an office in the Docks Office for its traffic manager and his staff from 1851, which was enlarged in 1857.

It has also been already noted that the SDC lent the LSWR money, and this favour was returned in 1853 when the LSWR lent the SDC £100,000 for future developments, which was converted into stock. Their close relationship was also seen in their joint opposition to any scheme that seemingly threatened their monopoly of trade, such as the 1856 proposal to build the broad gauge Salisbury and Southampton Railway to the Royal Pier.

The First Locomotive

In 1865 the LSWR and SDC also agreed to share the costs of an additional line into the docks for inward passenger trains. Later the same year there was another major development on the docks lines when, in November 1865, it was reported that a locomotive was working in the docks, which had been recently purchased by the SDC for £350. The locomotive was a vertical-boilered 0-4-0T built in 1861 by Chaplins of Glasgow, named *Chaplin*, and had been employed on the construction of the Bristol and South Wales Union Railway.

As a result of *Chaplin's* purchase the directors were told two horses had been dispensed with, and three more would go reducing the total to eight. However, at this

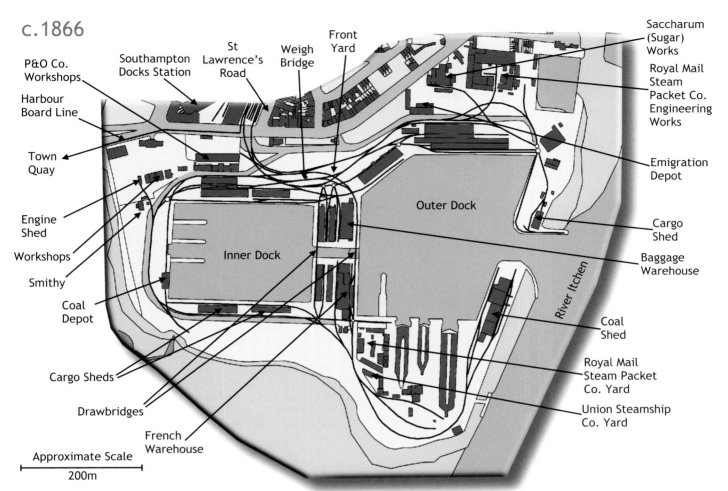

c.1866

P&O Co. Workshops

Harbour Board Line

Town Quay

Engine Shed

Workshops

Smithy

Coal Depot

Cargo Sheds

Drawbridges

French Warehouse

Southampton Docks Station

St Lawrence's Road

Weigh Bridge

Front Yard

Saccharum (Sugar) Works

Royal Mail Steam Packet Co. Engineering Works

Emigration Depot

Outer Dock

Inner Dock

Cargo Shed

Baggage Warehouse

River Itchen

Coal Shed

Royal Mail Steam Packet Co. Yard

Union Steamship Co. Yard

Approximate Scale

200m

time locomotive working would have been restricted as many lines were connected only by means of wagon turntables. There were also concerns from some quarters about the use of a steam engine in certain parts of the docks, with the SDC's insurers requesting a discussion on the use of the locomotive.

Further Growth

By this time the docks were a means of trans-shipping goods to many parts of the country, and by early 1886 the Great Northern Railway (GNR), the Great Western Railway (GWR), the London and North Western Railway (LNWR) and the Midland Railway (MR) all had offices on the docks estate. The growth in traffic led to the need for further sidings, and in March 1866 100 tons of rail was purchased for this purpose.

An order was placed for a second locomotive in 1866, which was supplied new by builders Henry Hughes and Co. of Loughborough. This was a 0-4-0 well tank built at a cost of £600 and named *Osborne*, which was delivered in September 1866, being first trialled on the 5th. It was not, however, a success, and, despite being converted to a saddle tank, it was sold in July 1872 for £450.

In April 1870 *Chaplin's* worn condition was giving cause for concern and so tenders for a new locomotive were invited. A quotation of £830 from Dick & Stevenson of Airdrie being accepted for an 0-4-0 saddle tank, which was delivered on 12th July 1870 named *Canute*. This

locomotive proved very successful lasting into LSWR service. It was not scrapped until 1903, having served as a stationary boiler for some years. *Chaplin* was sold in January 1872 for £150.

Strained Relations

Although the relationship between the LSWR and the SDC was close, it could get strained at times. Such was the case when the LSWR proposed a Bill for a new line into the docks in 1870. This would have run down the line of St Lawrence's Road across Canute Road and into the docks. In the end the bill was opposed by the SDC and eventually a compromise was negotiated.

Another source of tension between the two companies was the repeated complaints by the SDC of a shortage of wagons in the docks, which had been supplied by the LSWR. Therefore, in 1871 the SDC ordered their own wagons for internal use, with ten being delivered from the Metropolitan Railway Carriage and Wagon Co. of Birmingham at £46 10s each.

Increasing Traffic

In 1871 26,882 wagons loaded with cargo and 3,483 coal wagons were transported through the docks. This increasing traffic was taking a further toll on the permanent way with the renewal of six miles of the Company's lines being considered in May 1871.

In 1871 another locomotive was ordered at a cost of £829. *Sir Bevis* was another 0-4-0 saddle tank this time built by Shanks & Son of Arbroath and proved a success, also surviving into LSWR service. It was joined on 23rd July 1872 by a sister locomotive *Ascupart* from the same firm.

Further developments in the docks rail system were still taking place. The first signals appeared in 1872, controlling the crossing across Canute Road, and worked by the LSWR. Although new locomotives had been ordered still wagons were being moved by horses, and two replacement horses were also bought around this time.

Late in 1872 a new connection was laid to the terminus station, this time to the west of the existing lines, near the customs house, and was connected to Town Quay tramway. This is now the surviving connection across Canute Road. Meanwhile, in 1873, there was also additional rail accommodation provided at the Saccharum works at the north end of the docks estate where cane sugar was processed.

Itchen Quays

By this point the docks were being expanded again with the construction of the Itchen (or Extension) Quays between 1873 and 1876. The railway system was extended in turn, this time learning from previous experience with two lines between the cargo sheds and quays, and two lines in the sheds. Here the floors were built up to the level of the wagon floors, and there was also one line behind the sheds. In 1875 it was said that there were eight miles of track on the docks estate.

The original engine shed seems to have existed to the west of the Inner Dock as marked on an Ordnance Survey Map of 1870, and this was enlarged at a cost of £150 to accommodate more locomotives in 1871. When in 1878

two new locomotives were purchased the need for new accommodation became essential. Therefore, a new shed was built adjacent to the pumping house by Nos 1,2 & 3 dry docks. This location was now central to the docks rail network with the development of the Itchen Quays.

Vulcan Foundry in Newton-le-Willows supplied the two new locomotives. *Vulcan* arrived in the August and, like the previous docks locomotives, was an 0-4-0 saddle tank. It was joined in the November by *Bretwalda*, a near-identical sister. *Vulcan* survived into LSWR service but was laid aside by the SR on Grouping. *Bretwalda*, however, did see brief service for the SR.

New heavier locos, and increasing traffic meant that in 1879 the SDC asked for quotes for 200 tons of steel, as opposed to cast iron, rail to be obtained for replacements with the docks, with a quote of £8 5s per ton being accepted. A further supply was obtained in 1883 after the original stock was exhausted.

Further Threats

The 1880s saw further schemes for railways that the SDC opposed. First was the Didcot, Newbury and Southampton Junction Railway (DN&SJR), which proposed a new line running to the Royal Pier and then running powers over the docks lines. In truth one suspects that the SDC had mixed feelings over this proposal. They certainly did not like the thought of the DN&SJR having running powers over their lines, but probably the idea of a more direct route to the north with extra traffic potential was not unattractive. However, due to their allegiance with the LSWR they opposed the Bill. But when the Bill was finally passed in 1887 the powers for running on the Docks Co. lines had been struck out, and in the end the DN&SJR never built its line into Southampton.

Left: SDC locomotives *Canute* (on the left) and *Sir Bevis* (on the right) near the locomotive shed c1900. This sadly damaged image is one of the few photographs of either locomotive known.
(Photo: H. Brain Copyright NRM/SSPL)

Left: Manufacturer's photograph of *Vulcan* constructed for the SDC in 1878 by the Vulcan Foundry in Newton-le-Willows. It was joined at the docks by the near-identical *Bretwalda* later the same year. *Vulcan* was displaced by the B4s in 1900 and worked in a variety of locations, including back at Southampton, until it was sold in 1924. It was scrapped in 1931.
(Photo: *Southern Railway Magazine* Courtesy BRB)

The next scheme was the Swindon Railway Bill of 1883, which proposed the building of a line along the western shore of Southampton Water to a new port facility at Stone Point on the Solent. It was clearly not in the SDC's interest to have a rival port facility opened so close by, and so they opposed it, along with the later South Hampshire Railway and Pier Bill of 1885.

The Empress Dock

By 1884 the provision of further deep water berths was under discussion with Southampton Corporation. There was even talk of the Corporation lending the SDC £200,000 in order to build new facilities. In the end legalities meant this could not take place and it was suggested that the LSWR might do so instead. With the funding in place work on what would be the Empress Dock began.

As part of the new dock the SDC's engineer Alfred Giles devised a plan in January 1890 for five and a half miles of track to be laid around the new docks at a cost of £1,300 per mile. This included the purchase of 20,000 nine foot by ten inch by five inch sleepers, at a cost of 2s 9d each.

Originally it was envisaged that the north quay would be developed first, but economies in the scheme meant that it was the west quay sheds that were built first in May 1890, with lines being laid on the south quay in time for the opening on 26th July 1890. The north quay sheds and rail connections were completed in January 1891, while lines were laid around the whole dock by March 1891. They were stated to be 'practically finished' by the following month.

Meanwhile, work to renew the existing system continued with supplies of replacement rail being obtained in 1887, and 300 new sleepers in May 1888. Part of this work was relaying the connections to the Docks station to a 396ft radius curve. The curves on the docks line had always been a cause for concern for the SDC, who even wrote to the LSWR in May 1844 to enquire as to whether a 100ft radius curve was sufficient for the royal carriage.

Tenders were also invited in November 1889 for two new locomotives, with the order going to Hawthorn, Leslie and Co. for £1,990 for the pair. Once more they were to be 0-4-0 saddle tanks, but were significantly heavier than their predecessors. In January 1890 the SDC minutes stated that the new locomotives were to be named *Clausentum* and *Ironsides*, in the event when they were delivered in July 1890 *Ironsides* had become *Ironside*.

Left: SDC locomotive *Ironside* seen at Eastleigh.

(Photo: Bert Moody Collection)

c.1884

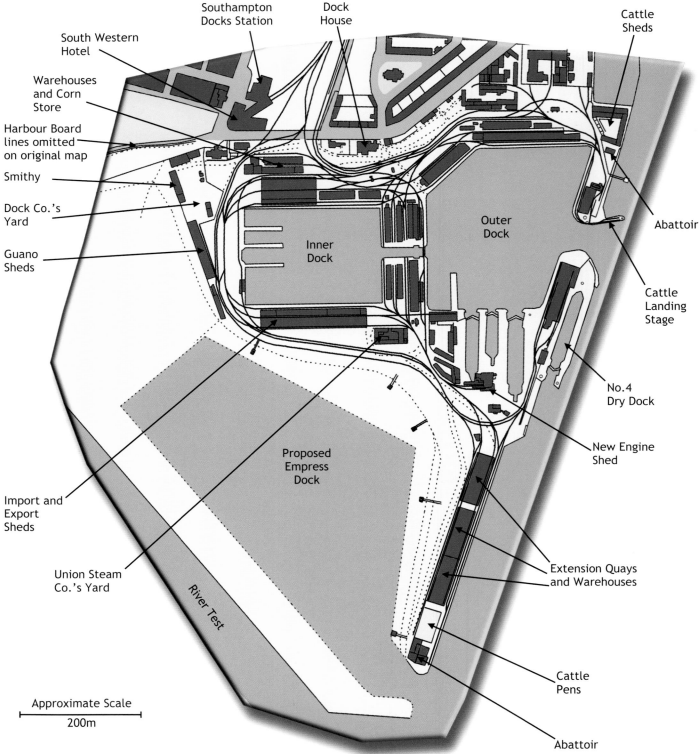

South Western Hotel

Southampton Docks Station

Dock House

Cattle Sheds

Warehouses and Corn Store

Harbour Board lines omitted on original map

Smithy

Dock Co.'s Yard

Guano Sheds

Inner Dock

Outer Dock

Abattoir

Cattle Landing Stage

No.4 Dry Dock

New Engine Shed

Import and Export Sheds

Proposed Empress Dock

River Test

Extension Quays and Warehouses

Union Steam Co.'s Yard

Cattle Pens

Approximate Scale

200m

Abattoir

Based on map produced for the French Ministère des Travaux Publics in 1884.

Above: A view taken from the Outer Dock of the grain elevator and warehouses on the north quay of the Inner Dock. In the foreground is one of the drawbridges across the link between the two docks. (LSWR postcard John Alsop Collection)

Takeover by the LSWR

The docks were taken over by the LSWR in 1892, who immediately set about completing the rail system around the Empress Dock, with the provision of new sidings on the north side, plus a weighbridge at a cost of £2,250. This was completed in 1893, and formed an extensive marshalling yard between the Empress Dock and the Inner and Outer Docks known as Empress Yard. The same year a new connection was made with the Harbour Board lines at the western end of the then docks estate, which enabled trains to and from Town Quay and Royal Pier to avoid travelling along Canute Road.

More new locomotives for the docks were also recommended and, in May 1893, a new 'tram' engine constructed at Nine Elms was said to be about to be trialled at the docks. If these were successful two of the new class would be transferred. These were members of the new class B4 0-4-0 tank locomotives, and by the November Nos. 81 and 176 were at work in the docks, later named *Jersey* and *Guernsey*. The following month they were joined by Nos. 96 and 97 which became *Normandy* and *Brittany* respectively. In addition to the locomotives several old wagons were also transferred in October

1893. Further B4s were transferred to the docks so that there were twelve of the class allocated there by 1901, with two of the similar K14 class added in 1908.

By April 1894 the state of the old SDC lines in the docks was giving concern, and so immediate improvements were authorised at a cost of £995. During the next couple of years the old SDC track was all relayed to the LSWR's standards, and by October 1895 it was said that £13,289 had been spent relaying just over nine miles of track.

However, by now the southern extension to the Itchen wharves was underway, and 100 tons of rail was ordered for the lines to serve these new facilities in February 1895. Half of this was in the form of flat-bottom rail for the quaysides, while the rest was 80 lb bull-head for the connecting lines. A further 101 24ft lengths of flat-bottom rail were ordered for the wharves in December

Above: Preserved nameplate of SDC locomotive *Clausentum* scrapped in 1945.
(Photo: Courtesy the late Frank Burridge Collection)

Lower: *Clausentum* at Eastleigh.
(Photo: Courtesy Bert Moody Collection)

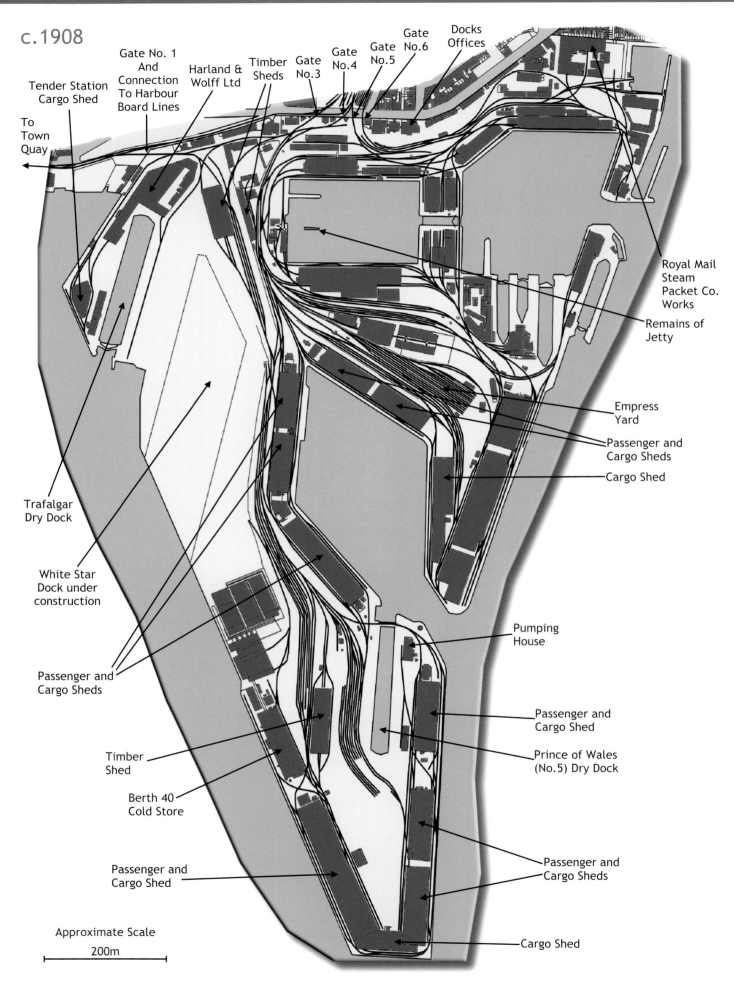

c.1908

To Town Quay

Tender Station Cargo Shed

Gate No. 1 And Connection To Harbour Board Lines

Harland & Wolff Ltd

Timber Sheds

Gate No.3

Gate No.4

Gate No.5

Gate No.6

Docks Offices

Royal Mail Steam Packet Co. Works

Remains of Jetty

Empress Yard

Passenger and Cargo Sheds

Cargo Shed

Trafalgar Dry Dock

White Star Dock under construction

Passenger and Cargo Sheds

Pumping House

Passenger and Cargo Shed

Prince of Wales (No.5) Dry Dock

Timber Shed

Berth 40 Cold Store

Passenger and Cargo Shed

Passenger and Cargo Sheds

Cargo Shed

Approximate Scale

200m

Above: This remarkable photograph shows the Front Yard at the docks in the early 1890s taken from above Dock House. An impressive array of ships is in the Outer Dock, while just to the left of the warehouse on the right the Inner Dock can be glimpsed between the buildings. Seen in the background is the chimney of the pumping house for Dry Docks 1, 2 and 3, behind which is the engine shed. Between the sheds in the centre background tarpaulined wagons can be seen. On the right is one of the docks locomotives, either *Vulcan* or *Bretwalda*. To its left is the weighbridge and associated hut, while behind it is an 18ft LSWR cattle wagon of 1880s design, while in front of it is a 24ft Passenger Luggage Van also of 1880s design. On the left, there appear to be three visiting covered vans. Interestingly the 'blurr' that can be seen above the middle van is a pair of horses hauling a wagon, demonstrating that horse power had not entirely been eliminated by this time.

(Photo: Courtesy Robert Pearl)

Summary of the History of the Docks Company's Locomotives

Name	Maker	Date Built	LSWR No(s).	SR No.	Left Docks	Disposal
Chaplin	Chaplin & Co.	1861	N/A	N/A	1872	Sold, then Unknown
Osborne	Henry Hughes	1866	N/A	N/A	1872	Sold, then Unknown
Canute	Dick & Stevenson	1870	N/A	N/A	1903	Scrapped 1903
Sir Bevis	Alexander Shanks & Son	1871	N/A	N/A	1903	Sold to C.D. Phillips of Newport
Ascupart	Alexander Shanks & Son	1872	N/A	N/A	1903	Sold to Australia
Vulcan	Vulcan Foundry Ltd	1878	118, 111, 0111	N/A	1900	Went to Poole Quay, and then various duties, sold 1924 to Taylor, Tunnicliffe and Co., Staffordshire, scrapped 1931.
Bretwalda	Vulcan Foundry Ltd	1878	408, 0408	E0408	1900	Used on construction projects, later as a pilot at Guildford and Nine Elms, sold in 1924 to J.R. Wood at Dibles Wharf, and scrapped in 1935.
Clausentum	Hawthorn, Leslie & Co.	1890	457, 0457	E734	1901	Served on Harbour Board lines until 1914, then various duties including Guildford pilot until scrapped in 1945.
Ironside	Hawthorn, Leslie & Co.	1890	458, 0458	E0458, 3458, 30458(BR)	1901	Served in various capacities including Guildford pilot until scrapped in 1954.

Above: Another early view this time looking north from the then newly opened Empress Dock c. 1900. This shows clearly that passenger operations were a major feature by the late 19th and early 20th centuries. One boat train is departing in the background probably having come up from one of the Itchen Quays, and appears to have two bogies in the coaching stock. Meanwhile on the quayside stands another rake of four-wheel coaches. In the centre behind the departing train is the coal drop for sorting coal, while an interesting feature is the wooden gates across the quayside on the left.   (LSWR postcard courtesy John Alsop Collection)

1895 as additional berths were completed.

In 1896 telephones were installed on the docks system for communication with the Docks station, while the need for additional sidings for the potato and other traffic was discussed in the May. Further extensions to the docks led to more additions to the system. In 1902 the South and Test Quays were opened, with their associated lines, which included lines into the cold store at berth 40 on the Test Quays.

The completion of the Trafalgar Dry Dock and a new timber depot west of the Inner Dock in 1905, led to a further extension of the trackage. At this point there were now thirty-one miles of track on the docks estate.

Of course construction of the new docks involved the use of contractors, who built their own temporary lines to carry materials to and from the construction site. They also employed their own locomotives for the purpose. For the building of the Empress Dock up to eighteen locos were used on the contract.

The final major expansion of the dock railways under the LSWR occurred with the opening of the White Star (later Ocean) Dock in 1911. After this the only significant change under the LSWR came with the laying of a second line of rails across Canute Road through Gate No.3 during World War One. This gave a total length of track in the docks of thirty-seven miles by the time of the Grouping in 1923.

Above: One of the first class B4 0-4-0 tank locomotives allocated to the docks was No. 176 later named *Guernsey*. It is seen here on 31st July 1930, still with the cutouts on the rear and front sheets of the cab. The device on the top of the boiler behind the dome was a water filter unit, which was fitted to all the docks locomotives by the SR starting from 1925.

(Photograph: Ken Nunn Copyright LCGB)

White Star Dock

The growth in the size of liners meant that new deep water facilities had to be built, and so in 1908 construction of what was initially known as the White Star Dock was started. The contractors were Messrs. Topham, Jones and Railton.

(All pictures on this page are commercial postcards from the John Alsop Collection)

Above: Something of the scale of the work can be observed in this photo with various steam cranes at work. Meanwhile in the background one of the contractor's Manning Wardle locomotives can be spotted.

Right: Hauling the spoil wagons from the bottom of the dock in May 1908.

Left: Tipping the spoil into ships for disposal in the Solent.

Above: Another interesting view looking west across the Front Yard from a newspaper illustration c.1907. In the centre is one of the class B4 tank locomotives, and in the left background are the grain warehouses on the north quay of the Inner Dock, behind which the top of the grain elevator can be made out. To the left is a wagon at the entrance to the export shed on the north-west quay of the Outer Dock. Dock House can be seen in the centre-right background, while on the extreme right is Canute Road with the South Western Hotel in the distance. The photograph was taken from the large cargo shed behind the north quay of the Outer Dock.   (Illustration from *The Black and White* newspaper)

Above: Another view probably also from the early twentieth century looking at the engine house for the pumps for dry docks Nos.1, 2 and 3, which can be seen behind and to the left of the engine house, with a ship occupying No.3 dock. To the right of the boiler house is the two-road engine shed, which was to remain until the Southern rebuilt it in 1935. A locomotive can just be made out in the left-hand entrance to the shed. On the left are some of the buildings associated with the dry docks such as a smithy. This photograph was probably taken from a hydraulic coal tip which existed on the north side of Empress Yard at the time.
(Commercial Postcard)

The Southern

Under the Southern there was a programme of improvements in the docks. On the north and north-west quays of the Outer Dock the sheds at berths 7,8 and 9 were rebuilt in 1924. While the following year a new continental cross-channel station was provided on the north quay of the Outer Dock. The timber shed at berth 45 on Ocean Dock was rebuilt to provide extra accommodation and a line laid inside in 1926. In the same year the roads in the docks were also formally named.

Other improvements included a new weighbridge to replace the 1868 one in the Front Yard, and a new running shed for the locomotives, still at the southern end of Nos. 1, 2 and 3 dry docks. This provided covered accommodation for nine locomotives, plus a coal stage, clinker bin, sand pit, sand drying room and mess room at an eventual cost of £2,090. It was completed by May 1935. However, by then the New Docks extension had been built along the north bank of the River Test, north-west of the Royal Pier. The construction of the New Docks will be dealt with in detail in the next chapter.

Within the New Docks estate eight new passenger and cargo sheds were built and an extensive system of tracks laid out. These were originally linked to the rest of the SR system via the Harbour Board lines, but from June 1935 a connection from Millbrook came into service. Behind the sheds there was a 759ft long carriage cleaning shed, which was built at a cost of some £42,700. This could accommodate a train of twelve bogie coaches on each of six lines, and was equipped with a sprinkler system.

To the west of the shed was the docks engineer's department yard, where the four docks engines that were usually assigned to the New Docks were based, although there was never a loco shed there. At the western end of the New Docks estate a 70ft 'Mundt' type turntable was constructed supplied by Ransomes & Rapier in 1935 at a cost of £1,585 (now preserved at the Didcot Railway Centre). Further sidings were also laid out behind berths 105 to 108. When complete some 26 miles of track were laid out within the New Docks.

With the addition of the New Docks there was the need for additional motive power at the docks. This was initially provided by the use of 'visiting locomotives', but in 1933 the first of four members of the D1 class 0-4-2 tank locomotives arrived. These had been designed by William Stroudley for the LSBCR, 125 of the class being built between 1873 and 1887. The locomotives allocated to the docks were Nos. B633, 2240, 2286 and 2359, although they had all left by the outbreak of war.

Above: On 25th June 1939 class D1 0-4-2T No.2286, originally built in 1879 and named *Ranmore*, stands with class B4 0-4-0T No.95 *Honfleur*. No.2286 had been allocated to the docks in 1934 and later had a varied career during the Second World War being based in Liverpool, as well as on the Longmoor Military Railway. It was scrapped in 1948. *Honfleur* was built in 1893 arriving in the docks in 1896 where it was to serve until 1947 when it was sold to the Ministry of Fuel and Power, being scrapped in 1957.
(Photo: H.W. Robinson Copyright J.F. Hyde Steam Archive)

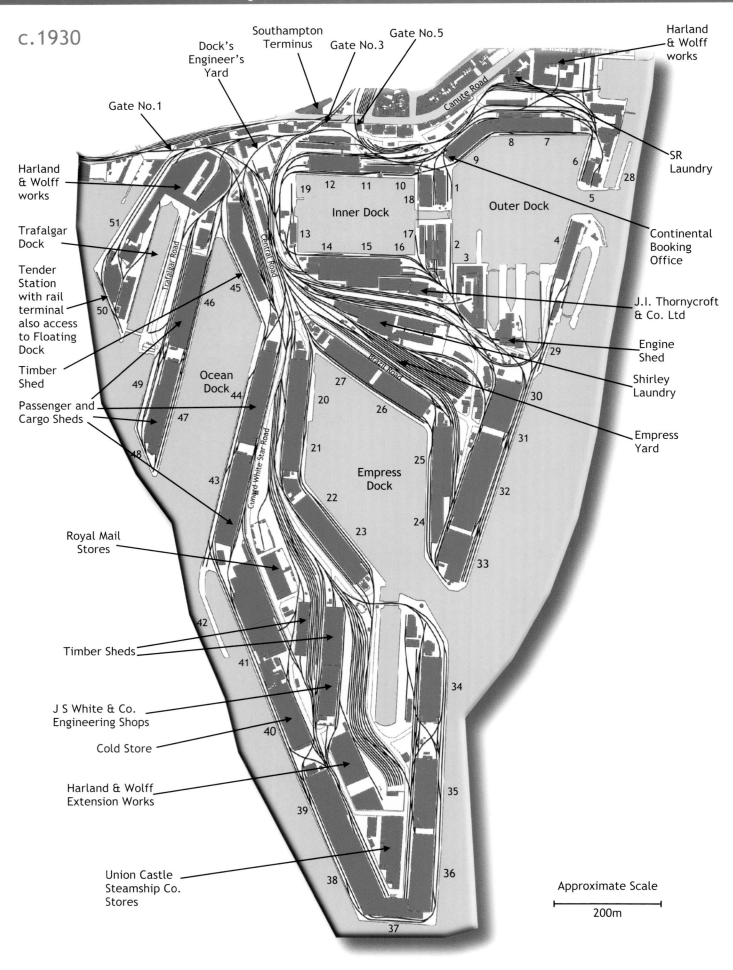

c.1930

Gate No.1

Harland & Wolff works

Trafalgar Dock

Tender Station with rail terminal also access to Floating Dock

Timber Shed

Passenger and Cargo Sheds

Royal Mail Stores

Timber Sheds

J S White & Co. Engineering Shops

Cold Store

Harland & Wolff Extension Works

Union Castle Steamship Co. Stores

Dock's Engineer's Yard

Southampton Terminus

Gate No.3

Gate No.5

Harland & Wolff works

SR Laundry

Continental Booking Office

J.I. Thornycroft & Co. Ltd

Engine Shed

Shirley Laundry

Empress Yard

Canute Road

Inner Dock

Outer Dock

Central Road

Trafalgar Road

Ocean Dock

Brazil Road

Cunard-White Star Road

Empress Dock

Approximate Scale

200m

19 12 11 10
18
1
13   17
14 15 16
2
3
4
5
6
7
8
9
28
29
30
31
32
33
34
35
36
37
38
39
40
41
42
43
44
45
46
47
48
49
50
51
20
21
22
23
24
25
26
27

Old Docks From The Air
One of the best ways to appreciate the complexity of the docks railways
(Ship's names, where known, in italics)

Looking North-West c.1930
(Commercial Postcard)

Looking North on 22nd August 1936
(Photo: Southern Railway Courtesy BRB)

Looking North-east Towards Terminus Station in the Early 1920s

Labels: Terminus Station Building, South Western Hotel, Terminus Goods Shed, Dock Gate No.3, Canute Road Crossing Box, Canute Road, Dock Gate No.5, Grain Store, Inner Dock, Customs House, To Dock Gate No.1, Trafalgar Dry Dock and Town Quay, Union Castle Offices, Board of Trade Offices, Docks Engineer's Yard, To Empress and Ocean Docks

Looking North Up Central Road Towards Queen's Park in the Early 1920s

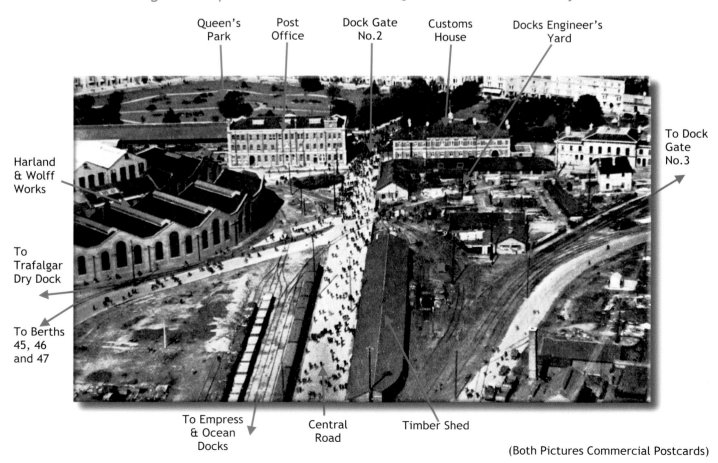

Labels: Queen's Park, Post Office, Dock Gate No.2, Customs House, Docks Engineer's Yard, To Dock Gate No.3, Harland & Wolff Works, To Trafalgar Dry Dock, To Berths 45, 46 and 47, To Empress & Ocean Docks, Central Road, Timber Shed

(Both Pictures Commercial Postcards)

Above: Ex-LSWR class B4 No.93 *St Malo* in the then recently rebuilt docks shed in 1936. The first eight B4s either constructed for, or transferred to, the docks were fitted with front and rear cab sheets with cut-outs to facilitate shunting. But from the early 1920s the front driver's cut-outs were filled in, and later the cabs were filled in with side sheets. The SR painted the docks B4s initially in lined green, but later some received a dark chocolate livery. (Photo: Copyright Colour-Rail 7318)

Above: No.85 *Alderney* in the Old Docks on 25th June 1939. It had been built in 1891 and transferred to the docks in 1900, with it and No.98 *Cherbourg* replacing the docks locomotives *Vulcan* and *Bretwalda*. *Alderney* survived at the docks until 1947 and was scrapped in 1949. (Photo: H.W. Robinson Copyright J.F. Hyde Steam Archive)

Left: On 7th August 1931 No.89 *Trouville* is photographed at the docks. Built in 1892 it was transferred to the docks in 1901, lasting there until the *USA* tanks arrived in 1947. In British Railways (BR) service it was number No.30089 serving as a shunter at Shoreham as well as at Plymouth, before acting as station pilot at Guildford.

(Photo: L. Hanson Copyright D. Hanson)

Above: B4 No.90 *Caen* was built in 1892 and transferred to the docks in 1901, having previously been based at Northam. It is seen here outside the docks shed on 25h June 1939. Reallocated from the docks in 1947 it was the first of the class to be withdrawn in 1948. The tower seen behind was part of the pump house for Nos.1,2 & 3 dry docks.

(Photo: H.W. Robinson Copyright J.F. Hyde Steam Archive)

Left: The maker's plate from No.97 *Brittany* scrapped in 1958. (Photo: Courtesy the late Frank Burridge Collection)

Right: It may look like a B4 but actually it is a later Drummond-built class K14, constructed in 1908, and seen here in 1924. It was numbered No.747 on the LSWR's books but named *Dinard*, in 1922 it was renumbered as No.147. *Dinard* lasted in service at the docks until 1947, and was then sold, working for the Blaenavon Co. Ltd until scrapped in 1958.
(Photo: H.C. Casserley)

Table of the History of the Class B4 and K14 Locomotives

No.	Built	To Docks	Name	Withdrawn	Disposal	Date Scrapped
81	11/1893	11/1893	Jersey	2/1949	Sold eventually to Skiningrove Iron Co., Saltburn	6/1961
85	10/1891	4/1900	Alderney	1/1949	Scrapped	7/1949
86	12/1891	2/1896	Havre	3/1959	Scrapped	3/1959
89	11/1892	3/1901	Trouville	3/1963	Scrapped	5/1964
90	11/1892	3/1901	Caen	5/1948	Scrapped	2/1950
93	12/1892	4/1896	St Malo	4/1960	Scrapped	5/1960
95	11/1893	2/1896	Honfleur	4/1949	Sold to Ministry Fuel and Power, Gwaun-cae-Gurwen, Swansea	10/1957
96	11/1893	12/1893	Normandy	10/1963	Sold to Corralls Ltd, now preserved at Bluebell Railway	N/A
97	11/1893	12/1893	Brittany	2/1949	Sold eventually to Stewart & Lloyds, Bilston, Staffs	8/1958
98	11/1893	5/1900	Cherbourg	2/1949	Sold eventually to Stewart & Lloyds, Bilston, Staffs	8/1958
102	12/1893	4/1896	Granville	9/1963	Sold to Butlins now preserved at Bressingham Museum	N/A
176	10/1893	11/1893	Guernsey	6/1948	Sold eventually to Stewart & Lloyds, Bilston, Staffs	2/1961
746 (later 101)	4/1908	4/1908	Dinan	11/1948	Sold to Taylor Woodrow	1/1954
747 (later 147)	4/1908	4/1908	Dinard	2/1949	Sold eventually to Blaenavon Company	8/1958

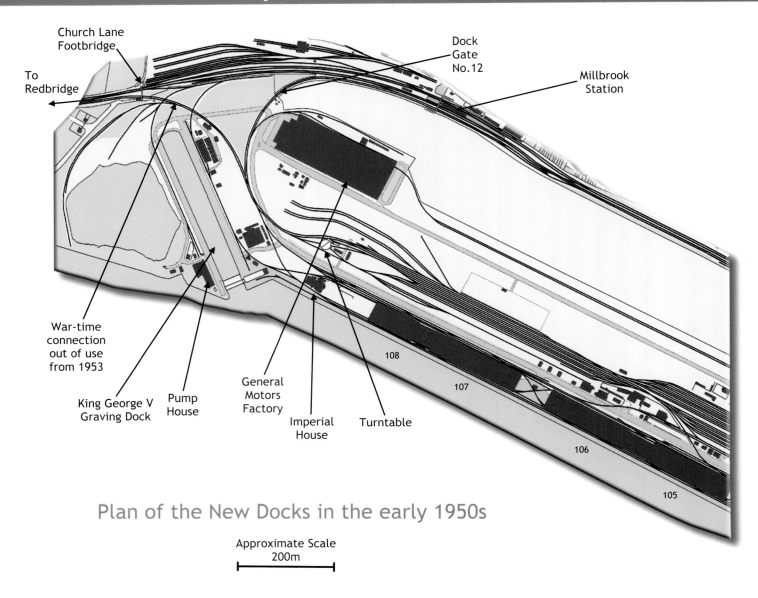

Church Lane
Footbridge

Dock
Gate
No.12

Millbrook
Station

To
Redbridge

War-time
connection
out of use
from 1953

King George V
Graving Dock

Pump
House

General
Motors
Factory

Imperial
House

Turntable

108

107

106

105

Plan of the New Docks in the early 1950s

Approximate Scale
200m

Left and Below: The Ramsomes & Rapier turntable in the Western Docks as seen on 12th August 1975. Not long after these photographs were taken the turntable was removed and subsequently installed at the Didcot Railway Centre. In the background can be seen the gantries which carried cables from the Standard Telephone and Cable factory to the cable-laying ships.
(Photos: R. Silsbury)

Right: Class K14 *Dinan* in the New Docks on 25th June 1939. *Dinan* was built in 1908 and allocated directly to the docks along with *Dinard*. Originally was numbered 746, but later became 101 in 1922. It remained at the docks until 1947 and was sold to Taylor Woodrow in 1949, finally being scrapped in 1954.

(Photo: H.W. Robinson
Copyright J.F. Hyde Steam Archive)

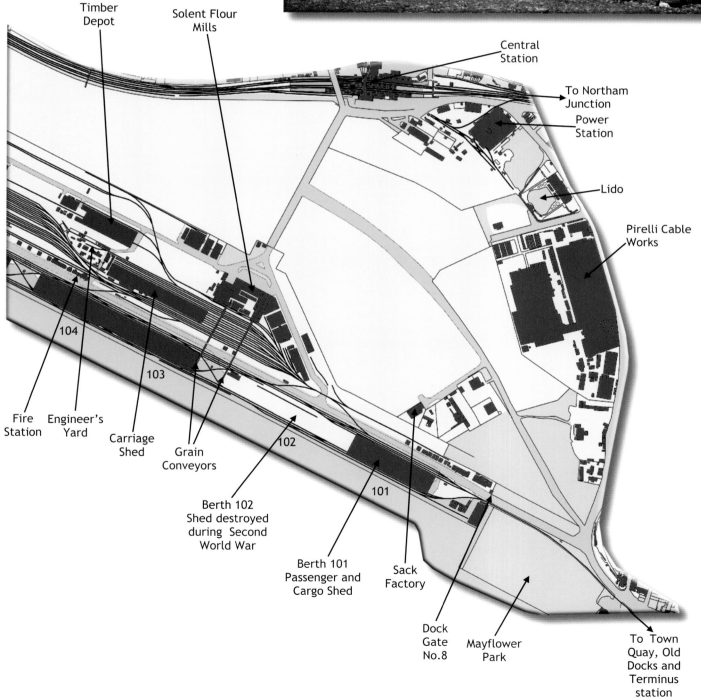

Timber Depot

Solent Flour Mills

Central Station

To Northam Junction

Power Station

Lido

Pirelli Cable Works

104

103

102

101

Fire Station

Engineer's Yard

Carriage Shed

Grain Conveyors

Berth 102 Shed destroyed during Second World War

Berth 101 Passenger and Cargo Shed

Sack Factory

Dock Gate No.8

Mayflower Park

To Town Quay, Old Docks and Terminus station

View Looking North-West Along Docks Extension On 22nd August 1936

(Ship's names, where known, in italics)

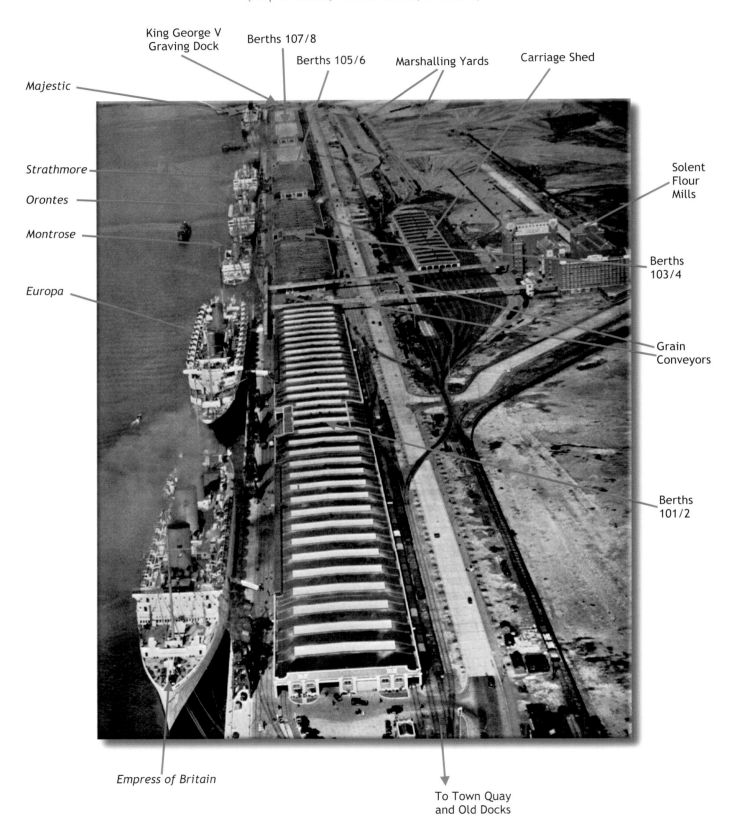

King George V Graving Dock

Berths 107/8

Berths 105/6

Marshalling Yards

Carriage Shed

Majestic

Strathmore

Orontes

Montrose

Europa

Solent Flour Mills

Berths 103/4

Grain Conveyors

Berths 101/2

Empress of Britain

To Town Quay and Old Docks

(Photo: Southern Railway Courtesy BRB)

Above: SR Class H15 No.524 built in 1924 at berth 101 on 15th October 1938. Moored at the quayside is the liner *Empress of Britain* with the liner *Europa* in the background.
(Photo: Copyright NRM and SSPL)

Below: The extent of the sidings in the New Docks can be judged in this photograph of *USA* tanks No.30062 in the background and No.30068 nearest the camera shunting in front of the Solent Flour Mills in April 1954. The conveyors to carry grain from ships to the mills can also be clearly seen.
(Photo: S.C. Townroe Copyright Colour-Rail BRS840)

Second World War

Following the completion of the New Docks there were no major developments in the railway system before the Second World War, save for connections being made to Rank's Solent Flour Mills, the Montague Meyer timber depot, the General Motors factory and other smaller factories, which were built on the New Docks Industrial Estate. During the war the railway infrastructure suffered during the bombing, but was largely kept operational. As the war progressed, particularly in the build up to D-Day, additional facilities were constructed, such as train ferry terminals at Mayflower Park adjacent to berth 101, by the Royal Pier, and also to the west of the King George V Dry Dock. There was also a new connection from Redbridge into the New Docks, so that trains could run in directly from the Bournemouth and Salisbury lines.

The preparations for D-Day put an immense strain on the railway system around Southampton including of course the docks. At the docks troops were also arriving by road, and so the competing traffic had to be co-ordinated. In the days following D-Day the railways transported reinforcements, but also started to carry incoming traffic including casualties and also prisoners of war. A train ferry service between Southampton and the newly-liberated port of Cherbourg was also established after D-Day (see page 122).

During the war additional locomotives were also allocated to the docks in the form of four ex-LBSCR class E1 0-6-0 tank locomotives Nos. 2112, 2156, 2162 and 2689.

After the War

Following the war there was a gradual return to peace-time operations. Equipment that had been destroyed by enemy action had to be replaced, and provision made for the repatriation of troops. On the docks railways the first Channel Islands boat train ran from Waterloo in June 1945, and later that year the first imported Guernsey tomatoes were unloaded for transporting inland. In the last week of August 1945 50,000 people passed through the port, most of these still service personnel, and it was not until 1947 that services to South Africa, Le Havre and St Malo were resumed.

By now the B4 tanks were in a poor state of repair, and in urgent need of replacements. They were heavily used, it was reported that the locos had run a total of 417,425 miles during 1935. Their replacements came in the form of 0-6-0 tank locomotives which had been shipped over for the US Army Transportation Corps, but had seen little service, being stored at Newbury Racecourse. A total of fifteen working locomotives were purchased, fourteen for the running stock and another for spares, coming into service in 1946 and 1947. These proved excellent machines on the tight curves of the Old Docks network.

However, a sign of things to come was the replacement of the Docks Engineer's Department steam locomotive *The Master General*. It had been purchased in 1928 to assist with the early stages of the New Docks development, but retained after the work was completed. However, in 1946 it was replaced by a Fowler 0-4-0 diesel-mechanical shunter.

Above: Q1 class C16 prepares to depart from the New Docks with a train of small US Army tanks which presumably had just been unloaded on 21st July 1943.
(Photo: Bert Moody Collection Courtesy BRB)

Left: During the last months of the Southern one of the 'Scottish' *Arthurs,* built by the North British Locomotive Company in 1925, No.771 *Sir Sagramore* backs through Empress Yard in the Old Docks on 17th May 1947.

(Photo: K.G. Carr Copyright P. Fidczuk)

Right: Departing through Gate No.5 possibly with a cross-channel boat train. *Lord Nelson* class No.863 *Lord Rodney* crosses Canute Road under the watchful eye of a flagman, and the not so great attention of two other members of staff.
(Photo:Copyright R.K. Blencowe Collection)

Left: Looking south from the deck of the SS *Shepperton Ferry* one of the train ferries used on the Dover to Dunkirk service, which had also seen service from Southampton during the war. Here it is in No.3 Dry Dock in 1948 with an unidentified class B4 on the quayside.
(Photo: S.C. Townroe Copyright R.K. Blencowe Collection)

Left: A number of the United States Army Transportation Corps 0-6-0 tank locomotives at the Newbury Racecourse 'dump'. They were originally built from 1942 as a shunter which fitted a European loading gauge. They were produced by three manufacturers Davenport, Porter and Baldwin, with the first being supplied to the British War Department as part of the 'lease-lend' scheme.

Later many were shipped to Europe following D-Day, but forty-two locomotives ended up at Newbury. It was from here that the fourteen locomotives, thirteen built by Vulcan and one by Porter were chosen for service at the docks in 1946. Later an additional Porter locomotive was purchased for spares. Nos. 1252 and 1254 eventually ended up in Yugoslavia, while No.1940 remained in the UK finally working at the Austin works at Longbridge. (Photographer Unknown)

Right: As part of the assessment before purchase No.4326 was taken on test to the docks in May 1946, and remained in service there. It is seen here under the grain conveyor at berth 103 in the New Docks. The two telephone kiosks, one at least out of service, are worth noting on the right. (Photographer Unknown)

Left: No.4326 was allocated No.74 by the SR, but was never repainted, retaining its US Transportation Corps livery and number until repainted by BR as No.30074 in October 1948.

It survived until 1965, when it was scrapped at Eastleigh having been transferred to departmental stock in 1963 as DS236. (Photo: Copyright R.K. Blencowe Collection)

Above: A *USA* class still in Southern livery shunts at the throat of Empress Yard. Behind is the towering presence of the *Queen Mary* which is berthed in Ocean Dock. This photo pre-dates the opening of Ocean Terminal in July 1950 on the left of the picture, as the *Queen* would be berthed there if the terminal was open. The last *USA* was repainted in BR livery in 1951.

(Photo: Lens of Sutton Association)

Above: *USA* class No.30071 pauses at the docks shed during the lunch break in January 1967. It would last in service until the end of steam in July 1967. Note the water hose for filling the loco tanks hanging in the entrance between the tracks. (Photo: T. Hastings)

Table of the History of the *USA* Class Locomotives

Works Number	Builder	US Army No.	SR No.	Into SR Service	BR No.	To Departmental Stock and No.	Withdrawn	After Withdrawal
7420	Porter	1264	61	11/1947	30061	10/1962 DS233	3/1967	Scrapped
4375	Vulcan	1277	62	5/1947	30062	12/1962 DS234	3/1967	Scrapped
4382	Vulcan	1284	63	10/1947	30063	N/A	5/1962	Scrapped after collision damage
4432	Vulcan	1959	64	6/1947	30064	N/A	9/7/1967	Preserved Bluebell Railway
4441	Vulcan	1968	65	11/1947	30065	11/1963 DS237	9/1967	Preserved Kent and East Sussex Railway
4377	Vulcan	1279	66	5/1947	30066	3/1963 DS235	c3/1965	Scrapped 8/1965
4380	Vulcan	1282	67	5/1947	30067	N/A	9/7/1967	Scrapped
4444	Vulcan	1971	68	10/1947	30068	N/A	3/1964	Scrapped
4425	Vulcan	1952	69	11/1947	30069	N/A	9/7/1967	Scrapped
4433	Vulcan	1960	70	4/1947	30070	8/1963 DS238	9/1967	Preserved Kent and East Sussex Railway
4439	Vulcan	1966	71	11/1947	30071	N/A	9/7/1967	Scrapped
4446	Vulcan	1973	72	4/1947	30072	N/A	9/7/1967	Preserved Keighley and Worth Valley Railway
4447	Vulcan	1974	73	6/1947	30073	N/A	12/1966	Scrapped
4448	Vulcan	4326	74	5/1946	30074	4/1963 DS236	8/1965	Scrapped 8/1965

Above: In 1946 the Docks Engineer's Department replaced their steam locomotive *The Master General* with a Fowler 0-4-0 diesel-mechanical shunter built in 1941. Originally it saw service at a Royal Ordnance factory in County Durham before being sold to the Southern. In the docks it was numbered 400S (later DS400) and is pictured here in the Engineer's Yard on 30th July 1952. It was sold in 1957.   (Photographer Unknown)

Nationalisation

On 1st January 1948 the docks and the railways became part of the nationalised British Transport Commission (BTC). The liner traffic gradually resumed through the 1950s with named boat trains being introduced in 1952. Meanwhile the flying boat service began to operate from its own purpose-built terminal with rail facilities at berth 50 from 1948.

Ocean Terminal was the next major piece of new infrastructure, opened on 31st July 1950, and able to accommodate two full length trains at any one time. Many of the photographs of the boat trains in the docks were taken at the Terminal, with enthusiast specials also visiting it as part of their itinerary.

During the 1950s there were further developments in the New Docks with a large Royal Mail Sorting Office established, as well as a submarine cable works owned by Standard Telephones and Cables. These also had rail connections.

Meanwhile ex-LBSCR class E1 and E2 0-6-0 tank locomotives were now employed in the docks to supplement the *USA* tanks, being used where the curves were more generous. In 1960 the allocation was two E1s and seven E2s. Class E4 0-6-2s were also seen at work in the docks, as well as class O2 0-4-4s and *Terrier* 0-6-0s.

By 1952 the rail network throughout the docks had reached 77 miles. However, this was the height of the system as gradually changes were taking place in the way both freight and passengers arrived and departed from the docks. This meant that while the total tonnages of freight handled have increased, the network of lines has gradually decreased. Change was also coming to passenger operations with the decline of the transatlantic liners, but the rise of the cruise ship.

In 1962 0-6-0 diesel shunters began to replace the steam locomotives in the docks. Fourteen were purchased new from Ruston & Hornsby for the purpose and were classified in the 07 class being numbered between D2985 and D2998, later becoming Nos. 07001 to 07014 under the TOPS classification. For a time steam and diesel were seen together, but the last members of the *USA* class to be assigned to the docks were soon transferred. However, they made frequent forays back onto the quaysides right up until the end of steam on the main line in July 1967.

Above: In July 1948 the Royal train makes its way past the Harland and Wolff works on its way to Ocean Dock headed by *Lord Nelson* class No. 30864 *Sir Martin Frobisher*. The workers are taking a keen interest as the train passes by. No.30864 is in one of the early BR liveries, with British Railways spelt out in full on the tender. (Photo: S.C.Townroe Copyright Colour-Rail BRS807)

Above: As stated in the text other classes of locomotives were allocated to the docks in the 1950s. Here class E1 0-6-0 tank locomotive No.32694 stands at the coal stage in the Old Docks, with the then new Thornycroft works building in the background.
(Photo: Copyright Colour-Rail 340024)

Above: In the New Docks classes E1 and E2 are seen together as E1 No.32689 and E2 No.32109 stand beside Herbert Walker Avenue with the Carriage Shed in the background. A MG 'ragtop' of early 1950s vintage is the foreground. No.32109 was allocated to the docks in 1956 and this photo probably dates from just after its arrival as it is still sporting the pre-1956 BR emblem. It lasted at the docks until 1962 and was withdrawn the following year.
(Photo: Copyright Colour-Rail BRS1762)

Above: On shed at the docks on 9th September 1965. By this time all the *USA* class locomotives were supposedly based elsewhere but two of them No.30071 on the left, and No.30073 in the shed, are back on duty there. On the right is class 07 D2989, which was supplied new to the docks in 1962. It lasted at the docks until 1977 when it was sold.

(Photo: H.W. Robinson Copyright J.F. Hyde, Steam Archive)

Right: Diesel shunter D2987 shunts at Ocean Terminal with the *Queen Mary* behind on 9th September 1965. D2987 later became No.07003 and was withdrawn and sold to industrial use in 1976. It was scrapped in 1985.

(Photo: H.W. Robinson Copyright J.F. Hyde, Steam Archive)

Above: Class 07 diesel shunter D2992 is shunting empty banana vans in the Eastern Docks in October 1967. D2992 was withdrawn in 1973 to be stored and scrapped in 1976.
(Photo: T. Hastings)

Above: On 20th May 1967 class 07 No.2991 hauls the empty stock from a boat train away from berth 30 with the *Nevasa* in the background. The *Nevasa* will be known to many school children in the 1960s and 70s from her role as an educational cruise liner before rising fuel costs led to its scrapping in 1975.
(Photo: John H. Bird Copyright Southern-Images)

Above: There were some unusual workings in and out of the docks. One such happened in spring 1967 when BR standard class 4 No.75068 arrived in the Eastern Docks with a gauge testing train.

(All Photos this page T. Hastings)

Above: Close up of DS22 *Gauge Testing Unit*. This was ex-South Eastern and Chatham Railway (SECR) composite lavatory brake No.1084, later SR No.3363, built in 1910. It was withdrawn in the late 1970s and is now based on the Bluebell Railway, where it re-entered service in October 2011 in a beautifully restored condition.

Left: The reason for the gauge train's visit became apparent a few days later when 4-TC set No.419 was brought into the docks powered by a class 33 'Crompton' diesel on a test run.

Decline and Partial Rebirth

Gradually the lines in the docks fell into decline as facilities were reduced. In the Eastern Docks (renamed in 1964) the closure and filling in of the Inner Dock led to the removal of the lines there. By the early 1970s the lines through Gate No.5 had been removed with the lines around the Outer Dock and on the extension quays also taken out of use or lifted. By 1972 the operations in the Eastern Docks declined to the extent that British Rail announced the withdrawal of freight working there.

By 1975 most of the lines of the Empress Yard had been lifted and the other yards had gone completely. The engine shed was also demolished the same year. At the same time the fleet of diesel shunters was also reduced until the last one was transferred in 1977, after this a loco was sent down from Eastleigh as required until the closure of the link line between the two docks in October 1979. After this trains were handled by main line locomotives.

The Eastern Docks system was reduced down to just a single line serving Ocean Terminal, before that was demolished, although the line remained open down to the Queen Elizabeth II terminal at berths 38/39. However, by the early 1990s the entire system in the Eastern Docks

was mothballed. But, as will be seen, in the 1990s boat trains were again run to the Queen Elizabeth II terminal. More recently in 2011 the track layout in the Eastern Docks was altered to permit the running of car trains, which is now a twenty four hour operation.

Meanwhile in the Western Docks, again renamed in 1964, the rail system had suffered a similar decline to that in the Eastern Docks, and with the rise in the container traffic during the 1980s most of the track was lifted. The last major use of the quayside lines was in the mid 1980s including the unloading of the new class 59 diesels, which were imported from Canada in 1986.

In the early 1990s trains only occasionally ventured into the Western Docks, but in the mid-1990s car trains began to run regularly, as well as gypsum and coal trains, although due to the state of the track at one time locos could not run-round their trains. An ANSA car terminal was built near the site of the old General Motors factory in the early 2000s. Behind berths 107/108 a container loading facility was created, which has recently been improved. However, a refurbishment of the Mayflower P&O terminal in 2003 resulted in the removal of the internal rail platform. A small outside platform remains, and some boat trains continue to run both to the Eastern and Western Docks as well as the occasional railtour.

Left: The scene showing the remaining line into the Eastern Docks in 1975 from the top of the former South Western Hotel. Ocean Terminal can be seen just left of centre towards the top of the picture.
(Copyright Bitterne Local History Society)

Right: The same scene as above taken in 2004, with the *Queen Elizabeth 2* in the background.
(Photo: J. Brown)

Left: Engines no more, a view of the interior of the now disused docks loco shed taken on 20th May 1975 shortly before demolition. (Photo: R. Silsbury)

Above: With the end of allocated shunters at the docks, shunting duties are now performed by main line locomotives. Here class 60 No.60075 shunts electric multiple unit No.316997 behind berths 106/7 on 16th July 2001.

(Photo: R. Silsbury)

Left: Class 47 No.47780 departs from the Eastern Docks with the Venice-Simplon Orient Express train forming a boat train bound for London Victoria on 22nd July 1995. The crossing gates stand open for the train to cross Canute Road while the former South Western Hotel dwarfs the train. (Photo: D. Purvis)

Below: Class 66 No.66046 prepares to enter the docks at Canute Road in October 2002 with the remains of Southampton Terminus station to the right and the rear of the former South Western Hotel in the background. (Photo: D. Purvis)

Building the New Docks

Construction of the New Docks was split into three stages, but in the end only the first two were completed. Stage one involved the reclamation and building of what were to become berths 101 to 104, north-west of the Royal Pier, while stage two was for four further berths, and also the construction of a new graving dock. After tendering was completed, Sir Robert McAlpine and Sons were awarded the contract for the new berths, while J. Mowlem & Co. along with Edmund Nuttall won the contract for the graving dock.

Dredging first of all had to take place in order for the work on the new berths to proceed. A start was therefore made on a new deep water channel in 1927. The soft silt of the river bed was dredged up and disposed of in the open sea. Then a layer of gravel was excavated and transported to the former train ferry jetty. From here it was transported by rail to a dumping ground. At the same time the line of the new quay wall was also dredged to remove the silt and leave a firm foundation.

The first stage of the new quay wall was between Town Quay and the Royal Pier, and from there to just beyond the old train ferry jetty. Gravel dredged from the deep water channel was first of all dumped from barges in order to build up a bank to low tide level. Then a 'Bankswell' machine was used to lift gravel to the top of the growing bank.

Now sand and clay dredged from the deep channel could be pumped in the form of a slurry into the reclaimed area to raise the land level, at the same time allowing surplus water to escape, so that permanently dry land appeared. In order to form the quay wall 45ft square concrete 'monoliths' were used which were sunk into the river bed, and built up to the desired level. The first of these was lowered into place in February 1929.

This created an area which became the base for further construction. Here an extensive storage facility was set up with supplies for the on-going reclamation. In addition an extensive rail network was laid out connected to Terminus station via the Harbour Board lines and the Old Docks. As part of the building of the new quay wall the old toll house for the Royal Pier had had to be demolished as it lay in the path of the new rail connection to the Old Docks. It was replaced by a new building in cast concrete, built at a cost of £11,561, which still stands today. At the same time work was now proceeding on building the new quay wall north-west along the River Test.

Meanwhile a wooden trestle bridge was being constructed out to meet the new quay wall, from a point on the shoreline about half a mile west of Southampton West station. This consisted of wooden piles driven into the river bed. On top of the trestle a set of rails was laid, along which wagon loads of chalk excavated from the quarry at Micheldever were run and the chalk shovelled by hand from the wagons to form a bank. When the two banks nearly met a 'sluice gate' system was created using wooden gates between steel piles to 'seal' the area to be reclaimed. Then the pumping of the clay and 'slurry' into the resulting lagoon could begin, creating just under 200 acres of reclaimed land. The surplus water being allowed to escape through the sluices.

In November 1930 the second stage of the scheme was authorised, and the quay wall was now extended to a full 7,542ft length, with berths 105 to 108 being built. For this entire scheme McAlpine developed an extensive rail system as construction proceeded, with up to fifteen locomotives at work on the site at any one time. The first ship to use the new berths was the *Mauretania* on 19th October 1932.

Southampton West Station   Southampton Power Station

Right: A forgotten landscape; this is the view from opposite the Royal Pier in the early 20th century. All the water in the photo is now reclaimed land. Southampton Power Station and the West station can be seen in the distance.
(Colourized commercial postcard)

Above: This photo shows some of the early days of the work on the New Docks. Taken from the old town walls, in the centre is the former train ferry jetty, now used as a base of operations. To the left the new sea wall extends south-east to the Royal Pier, while the new wall is being built on the right. The methods used are described in the text. Material from the dredging was transported back from the jetty to a dumping ground inland. Note the track still in place on the jetty, and also that the signal and signal box are still in-situ. (Photo: Copyright Southampton Record Office/Associated British Ports)

Above: One of the land discharging dredgers in action on the New Docks extension. These machines could take material from barges and fill across walls or onto land. In this case it is depositing on the far side of the new sea wall that is being formed. (Photo: Copyright Southampton Record Office/Associated British Ports)

Aerial View taken in late 1920s of Stage One
(Photographer Unknown)

Train Ferry Jetty

Wooden Pier and Pile Driver

Chalk Embankment

Main line to Bournemouth

Southampton West station

Power Station

Town Quay

Royal Pier

New Royal Pier Entrance

Pirelli Cable Works

Lido

Right: A close-up of the contractor's base on what would later become Mayflower Park. The temporary jetty in the top left of the photo is worth noting, plus the track which almost makes a complete loop around the site.

Above: A near ground-level view of progress on the first phase of the New Docks taken from what would later become Mayflower Park. (Photo: Copyright Southampton Record Office/Associated British Ports)

Above: The new carriage shed is ready for trains. Interestingly near the foot of each of the columns between the tracks and at each end there are signs with the names of various shipping lines, in this photo they are from left to right: Orient Line, Norddeutscher Lloyd, French Line, Union Castle Line, Cunard White Star, P&O, United States Line. As there are more nameboards than tracks in the shed possibly these were removable and referred to the destination of the carriages on a particularly shed road that day. During 1935 11,434 coaches passed through the shed over the year.

(Photo: Copyright Southampton Record Office/Associated British Ports)

Above: An interesting comparison to the view on page 53 with the first phase of the New Docks in operation, although work is still continuing on the reclamation and on further berths in the background. Meanwhile a class T9 makes its way from the New Docks past the contractor's yard along the link line to the Harbour Board lines and Terminus station with a short train.
(John Alsop Collection)

Left: Compare the scene above to the photo on the left, taken in March 2012 from the section of the old walls seen in the bottom right of the picture above, with not a rail line in sight.

Right: An aerial view of the New Docks shortly after completion showing the George V Graving Dock with the *Queen Mary*. Millbrook station and goods yard can be seen, along with its good shed. The large General Motors factory can also be observed on the docks estate.
(Photo: Southampton Record Office/Associated British Ports)

The King George V Graving Dock

In November 1930 it was still undecided as to where the new graving dock was to be built, with Woolston still being a possibility. However, by June 1931 Millbrook had been decided upon and the contract given jointly to John Mowlem and Edmund Nuttall for the construction of a 1,200ft long by 135ft wide dry dock. Then the largest in the world, the first stage of this was the construction of a sea wall from alongside Millbrook station out into the river. A second wall was also built from Millbrook Point to join the first east of the site of the new dock to permit the reclamation of approximately 160 acres of land behind.

At the dock site itself deep wells were sunk to lower the water table, and excavation of the dock begun. Forty-three one foot wide trenches were dug for the walls, while the floor consisted of a 25ft thick layer of concrete. One and a quarter million tons of earth had to be excavated. Again an extensive network of rail lines was built with a total of eighteen locomotives employed on the contract.

In July 1933 the sea-wall that had sealed the end of the dock was removed and the entrance dredged, so that the dock could be officially opened by King George V on 26th July. However, the dock was not finally completed until the steel cassion gate was put in place. The *Majestic* was the first ship to use the dock in January 1934. Railway tracks ran from each side of the dock to connect with rest of the New Docks system.

Left: One of the Hunslet 0-6-0 saddle tanks supplied new to contractor J. Mowlem in 1931 for the dock construction. Named *Grosvenor* it was transferred to Norfolk in 1935, and then sold to the British Sugar Corporation at Cantley, where it is seen here. It was scrapped in 1958.

(Photographer Unknown)

Below: A view of the nearly completed graving dock with the crowds waiting in the grandstands for the royal yacht to break the ribbon at the entrance as part of the official opening on 26th July 1933. Some of the contractor's lines can be seen on the right. In the top right of the picture a line-up of locomotives, such as the one in the photograph on the left, can be observed. Millbrook station goods yard is the distance and the Church Lane footbridge can be seen above the top left hand edge of the dock.

(Commercial Postcard)

Scenes from the King George V Graving Dock Construction

Top: A jetty was built to allow spoil from the excavation to be loaded into barges for disposal. Here one of Mowlem's Hunslet locomotives can be seen with a train of tippers.

Centre: A train of cement is drawn past Millbrook goods yard on the left as seen from the Church Lane footbridge. It is worth noting the number of lines on the right, all part of the construction site.

Below: A scene showing the early stages of the excavation. The design of some of the cranes is worthy of note.

(All photos this page from *Southern Railway Magazine* courtesy BRB)

Goods Operations

Above: On 10th March 1962 class S15 No.30508, built in 1920, eases into the docks estate through Dock Gate No.3 having crossed Canute Road with a mixed goods train. No.30508 lasted in service until November the following year when it was withdrawn and scrapped.   (Photo: L.E. Elsey Copyright Colour-Rail 342025)

Early Days

At the outset the main use envisaged for the docks railways were for the handling of goods. This was not only for import and export, but also for transfer between ships along the quayside tracks.

At first goods were simply loaded into wagons, supplied by the LSWR, on the quaysides (see page 17) which were then hauled by horses to the required destination. This work was undertaken by the Docks Company's own workers, the LSWR only being involved when wagons were transferred to LSWR metals. But from 1855 it was proposed that the LSWR appointed clerks and foremen to oversee the loading. It was stated at the time that up to a dozen wagons could be being loaded in various parts of the docks simultaneously.

The demand for wagons led to an on-going complaint by the SDC of a lack of wagons in the docks, first mentioned in 1853, and continuing until the SDC decided to order their own wagons in 1871. At this point most wagons were of the open type, which were suitable for the goods coming through the docks at this time.

Timber was an early traffic, with a timber yard being established at the northern end of the docks estate in the

1840s, along with a timber pond in what would later become the coal dock. Later timber sheds and a yard were developed to the west of the Inner Dock.

Imported grain was also a significant traffic, the Inner Dock being set up to handle this trade with large grain warehouses built on the north quay. Coal was also handled through the docks, both for distribution in the local hinterland, and also for the supply of the steamships that used the port. This was brought in by coastal steamers with a coal depot in the Inner Dock.

Supplying the steamships also provided other loads to be carried on the docks lines. In 1854 the LSWR authorised the construction of two 'platform' wagons for the transport of propellers and other large machinery for the ships. It is not certain what sort of wagon was used to transport a hippopotamus to London in July 1854, but a newspaper report of the event records that the animal and its tank were secured to a wagon for the journey.

Potatoes and tomatoes from the Channel Islands provided seasonal traffic, while the cross-channel services also led to the import of produce from France. Another trade with the Channel Islands was in cattle and sheep with large pens and sheds established at the north-east corner of the Outer Dock. These would have been transported from the docks in cattle trucks, which were at first open wagons with built up sides and ends. Only in the 1860s did the LSWR introduce covered cattle trucks.

However, from 1866 to prevent the spread of Rinderpest it was required that all imported animals be slaughtered at the port. Therefore, an abattoir was also provided next to the cattle sheds at the north-east corner of the outer dock, and six cattle trucks were converted to meat vans for this trade. A second slaughter house was built at the southern end of berth 33 when the Itchen Quays opened in the 1870s.

Gradually, as services developed from the port to more far-flung parts of the world, other traffic became established. In 1871 26,882 wagon loads of cargo passed through the port as well as 3,483 wagon loads of coal.

Under the LSWR

The takeover of the docks by the LSWR in 1892, shortly after the Empress Dock was opened, led to the opportunity to develop new traffic and the need for specifically designed railway wagons for these goods. This was nothing new. The LSWR's first covered vans had been built in 1851 for the conveyance of 'specie', a collective term used for valuable items and bullion, which were imported and exported from Southampton from its earliest days.

One of the LSWR's first actions, in 1893, was to address the SDC's on-going complaint of a shortage of wagons in the docks. This they did by ordering the construction of fifty wagons. These were platform trucks, made from 'old materials', which would have been adequate for the transfer of goods on the low speeds of the docks lines. Another fifty wagons and two 'lock-up' vans were supplied in 1896, while in 1899 an order was placed for a hundred five-plank wagons, again for use in the dock. However, it is probable that many of the wagons that ended up at the docks were actually older or damaged ones from elsewhere.

Changes in technology also led to the need for new wagon designs. In the late nineteenth century the development of refrigeration on ships for the transportation of frozen meat, meant that this meat had to be carried from the docks in its frozen state after unloading. Therefore, in 1893 the LSWR constructed twenty 'refrigerated' vans for use in this growing trade from the docks. The refrigeration was achieved by the use of ice boxes at each end of the vans accessible through the roof. Later further batches of these vehicles were produced, particularly when the cold store was constructed at berth 40 in 1900, increasing the amount of frozen meat handled.

At the same time the LSWR, in anticipation of increased meat trade from America, also ordered fifty ordinary meat vans. They also engaged in an innovation, which in many ways could be described as the 'proto-containerisation' of the meat trade. This involved the construction of fifty horse-drawn meat wagons, and fourteen long van trucks, each capable of having two of the horse-drawn vehicles loaded on it. At the docks the wagons were filled with meat, and then loaded onto the trucks for transport to London. Having reached the capital the wagons were unloaded from the trucks, horses harnessed to them, and then drawn through the streets to various destinations across the city.

Another import through the docks which resulted in the building of more specialist vehicles was the grain trade. For this 20 wooden 10 ton 'Hopper' wagons were ordered in 1896, possibly to supply the Huntley and Palmers factory at Reading. These were delivered in 1898 at a total cost of £1,200.

The LSWR improved cargo handling throughout the docks including the provision of electric lighting, along with hydraulically operated, and later electrically operated, cranes, along with steam-powered travelling cranes. They also installed a grain elevator on the north quay of the

Left: In the early years of the 20th century, a scene showing the hand-loading of meat into one of the LSWR's refrigerated vans. The sign on van No.12606, constructed in 1900, states that it contains 'Reformer Argentine Chilled Beef'. At the head of the vans is one of the class B4 shunters.
(Photographer Unknown Courtesy *The Railway Magazine*)

Above: Headed by *Trouville* a train of meat wagons, loaded onto platform wagons ready to be transported to London is seen on the quayside.

(Postcard from the John Alsop Collection)

Right: Unloading the meat wagons from the flat trucks at their destination whilst a team of horses wait patiently to be hitched to the wagon.

(Photo: Southampton Record Office/Associated British Ports)

Left: As trade through Southampton grew the number of places goods travelled to and from on the mainland increased. This is reflected by the variety of wagons from different companies that could be seen in the docks. This view, which dates c.1912, was taken from the Inner Dock looking west across the White Star Dock. A wide variety of rail wagons can be observed including those of the Great Western Railway and Great Northern Railway. The shed in the picture was for storing timber, while in the background the chimney belongs to the pumping house for the Trafalgar Dry Dock.

(Commercial Postcard)

Left: Behind the warehouses at berths 34, 35 and 36 in 1926 the Southern installed two travelling gantry cranes, known as 'Goliath' cranes, for the loading and unloading of wagons into the warehouses at a cost of £1,040 each. They are seen here in this photo which features two wagons still in LSWR livery and a Great Western open wagon.

(Photo: Southern Railway Courtesy BRB)

Inner Dock and built new accommodation for the shunters. These shunters were responsible for the marshalling of trains in the docks ready for despatch.

By the summer of 1913 there were trains on weekdays at 6.00 pm, 7.55 pm, and 9.35 pm to London (Nine Elms), a 4.00 pm train to Willesden, and a 9.58 pm train to Eastleigh. In addition there was a path for a train of perishable traffic from the Channel Islands for use when required at 10.05 pm to Waterloo, with the instruction that every effort should be made to give this a clear run.

Grouping and the Southern

By 1922, just before the LSWR became part of the SR, the annual tonnage of cargo dealt with at the port was 433,211 tons imported and 309,623 tons exported, most of which would have been transported on the docks

railway system. However, one of the first acts of the SR on taking over responsibility for the port was to drop the rates charged to shippers by 10% to encourage more trade.

As already noted too, further battery powered tractors were purchased to assist in the movement of goods around the docks. Two 'Goliath' cranes were also installed at the rear of the warehouses at 34, 35 and 36 berths to load rail wagons directly from the warehouse.

At this point the cargo handling at the docks was divided into distinct areas. The Outer Dock warehouses handled coffee, cocoa, dried fruits, tobacco, cigars and wine, those in the inner dock dealt with grain, timber and fruit. The latter was mainly handled at berths 14, 15 and 16, with an auction house established in the warehouse at berth 14.

Left: *Trouville* again on 3rd September 1937 shunting in the Old Docks past the United States Lines offices at Ocean Dock.
(Photo: Bert Moody Collection)

Above: The Southern advertised Southampton at various times as *The Gateway of* (or *to*) *the World*. It is interesting looking at the range of flags for the nations which traded with Southampton in the 1930s. Many flags are still in use, while others, as in the case of the Nazi flag, thankfully are not.
(Poster Courtesy the late Frank Burridge Collection)

The Empress Dock was used for troop embarkation, but berths 21 to 27 were also the berths of the Royal Mail Steam Packets to South America. Meanwhile berths 30 to 33 on the old extension quay handled a number of boats from different companies trading with the Far East. Berths 34 through to 41 were extensively used by Union Castle for their South African and continental services. The berths in Ocean Dock were primarily used by the North American liners, although berth 45, as already stated, was set up to handle timber.

However, the major development came with the docks extension. Here the new berths were laid out with ease of handling both passengers and cargo very much in mind. The railway system in particular was a much improved development of the haphazard growth of the lines in the Old Docks.

There were rails along the quaysides, and lines running into the passenger and cargo sheds, as well as along the rear of the sheds. Meanwhile the provision of crossover tracks between pairs of berths gave easy access for trains to the quayside. In addition, there were extensive

marshalling yards, plus rail access at either end to either Millbrook, or to Terminus station via Town Quay. All of this led to a very efficient system for handling goods.

Some idea of the amount of rail traffic dealt with at the docks comes from figures given out at the Docks Traffic Controller's Annual Dinner early in 1935. Here it was stated that in 1925 272,000 wagons were dealt with at the docks. By 1934 this had risen to 289,000, despite the depression, and with the New Docks only partially opened in the August. In all during the first eleven months of 1934 3,760 goods trains were dispatched, an average of almost eleven a day. However, by 1936, when the New Docks were fully operational, the figures had risen to 324,000 wagons dealt with and 4,245 freight trains dispatched, approaching twelve trains a day. This showed the effect the New Docks had. Pre-war cargo traffic peaked in 1937 at approximately 1.3 million tons for the year.

Of course, as has been seen, the war brought many challenges to the handling of goods through the port, particularly with the dispatch of the Expeditionary Force to France, and the run up to D-day. However, there was a period in 1940-1 when virtually no cargo passed through the docks. By 1942 about 600,000 tons of goods were handled. This decreased slightly in 1943, but 1944 was the peak year of the war with approximately two million tons of cargo dealt with.

Post-War Nationalisation

With the end of the war initial concentration was on the rebuilding of the structures that were lost, but plans were also drawn up for new facilities. However, as has been seen some of these, such as the new 'super' warehouse, did not come to fruition.

The period following nationalisation saw a move towards the bulk handling of goods. Increasingly goods arrived and departed from the docks by road as opposed to rail. It is not, therefore, surprising that the docks' railways began to enter a period of gradual decline through the 1960s, which accelerated through the 70s and 80s with the removal of much of the rail system in the Eastern Docks.

However, there was still substantial traffic, and on Mondays to Fridays in the summer of 1963 goods trains arrived at the docks from Eastleigh at 2.08 am, 3.53 pm, and 10.56 pm. From Nine Elms the arrivals were 3.42 am (except Monday), 4.21 am, and 10.40 pm, and from Feltham at 4.52 am (Monday excepted), 7.56 am (Monday only), 9.50 am (Monday excepted).

Departing trains the same summer left for Feltham at 4.24 pm; Eastleigh at 12.30 am and 6.30 pm; Salisbury at 6.05 pm; Nine Elms at 6.50 pm and 11.00 pm; Crewe at 7.00 pm; Northam Yard at 9.00 pm; Brighton 9.30 pm (when required); and Bevois Park Yard at 10.30 pm. In addition, there were a number of timetabled paths available between midnight and 12 noon for trains to be run to Nine Elms, Feltham, Exeter, Romsey, Woodford, Salisbury, and Temple Mills as required. All incoming and outgoing trains were routed via the Old Docks.

By October 1968 most trains were still routed into the Eastern Docks with up to nine paths available from South Lambeth, Northam, Washwood Heath, Eastleigh and Banbury. Up to eight paths were available out from the Eastern Docks to Northam, Healey Mills, Bevois Park, and Bescot, most to be used as required. From the Western Docks there were up to eight paths per day available. These included three scheduled departures at 6.15 pm to South Lambeth, 6.30 pm to Bescot, and 6.44 pm to Eastleigh. There was also another path available to Feltham that could run from either the Eastern or Western Docks.

Containerisation

The big change to the way bulk goods are handled at the docks was the rise of containerisation. As has been mentioned, the concept of containerisation was not new, with the LSWR's use of wagons on trucks as a means to speeding the handling and delivery of meat in London in the late nineteenth and early twentieth centuries.

Above: Class E2 No.32103 shunts berth 20 at the Empress Dock on 26th April 1962. The fine array of cars parked beside the line are worth noting.
(Photo: Colin Hogg Copyright Bluebell Railway Museum Archive)

Above: *USA* tank No.30072 is shunting in the Front Yard near the cross-channel terminal on 18th June 1955. The number 9 on the front is the duty number for the day.
(Photo: Peter T. Hay)

Above: Not yet a year old BR Standard class 4 2-6-0 No.76068 completed in August 1956 is seen departing from Empress Yard with a freight train on 26th June 1957. Sadly this loco was not even going to last a decade, being withdrawn in 1965 and scrapped the following year. In the background the Royal Fleet Auxiliary Tanker *Tide Austral* is tied up at berth 20.
(Photo: R.C. Riley Copyright Transport Treasury)

Elsewhere general goods containers were being developed, with the Railway Clearing House (RCH) setting standards in the 1920s for the sizes of containers to be used, which could be lifted on and off trucks by crane.

In 1928 the SR introduced insulated containers, again primarily for the meat traffic between Southampton Docks and London. These were 11ft 8¾in long and 5ft 7⅝in wide and 6ft 6in high, designed to carry a load of up to three and a half tons. Insulation was provided by means of sheets of cork in the sides, ends and roof, while the floor was lined with asbestos. They could be mounted on a flat-bed wagon for rail transportion and then lifted onto the back of a lorry for delivery to their destination. These were also used for transporting bananas and eggs to and from the continent.

It was after the Second World War that containerisation began to take-off with the use of 8ft by 8ft containers with lengths in 10ft units. This led to the development of the container berths at Southampton in the late 1960s and early 1970s. However, a marked change with the previous practice of handling goods at the docks was that rail tracks no longer ran to the quaysides in the container terminal. Instead containers are moved by self-propelled vehicles around the quayside, and transported to the Maritime Container Terminal on the south-west side of the Bournemouth line between Millbrook and Redbridge for transfer to rail.

However, more recently a new container 'pad' has been established behind berths 107/8 to allow the loading and unloading of containers there as well. All of this means that today the amount of cargo handled by rail to and from the the port greatly exceeds that transported over the docks lines in the heyday of the system. In total over 39 million tons of cargo passed through the port of Southampton in 2010, a substantial portion of which still commenced or completed its journey by rail.

Left: A Southern Railway Insulated Container compete with meat hooks loaded on a Conflat 'B' wagon.

(Photo: Southern Railway Courtesy BRB)

Below: Class E1 No.32694 shunts two RCH containers chained to flat wagons in the New Docks on 22nd April 1960.

(Photo: Dave Cobbe Copyright RailPhotoprints)

Above: A new container 'pad' was established in the Western Docks to permit the loading of trains at the back of berths 107/8. Here EWS class 67 No.67006 *Royal Sovereign* is seen with a train on 27th March 2007.   (Photo: D. Purvis)

Above: On 19th January 2011 EWS class 66 No.66146 exits from Western Docks to join the main line at Millbrook with a modern container train.

Goods Handled

It is now worth spending some time considering how specific cargoes were handled as the docks developed. The tables on page 70 shows the principal cargos which passed through the docks in 1927. Some of these were obviously more significant than others, and some are now lost in the mists of time.

Grain

As has been stated the import of wheat grain was a significant traffic through the port. The installation of a grain elevator by the LSWR in the Inner Dock, capable of handling 75 tons per hour, bears testament to this. There was also the provision of the especially designed hopper wagons. As a further development when the SR started work on the New Docks one of the key components was what was to become known as the Solent Flour Mills.

Built by Joseph Rank Ltd on a two acre site, construction of the mills started in late 1932, and they were opened in 1934. They stand behind berths 102 and 103, and grain was raised from ships' holds by means of pneumatic suction, then transported directly into the mills on conveyors. Therefore, the grain was never transported by the railway system, only the processed flour was dispatched by train being carried in sacks in wagons.

The mills were severely damaged during the Second World War and had to be rebuilt, becoming operational again in 1951. They were extended in 1955, and new grain silos added in 1964. Today the mills are still in operation, but there is no longer a rail connection, which is also the case with another grain terminal opened at berth 36 in 1983.

Timber

Like grain, timber was an important commodity from the earliest days. Most timber would originally be unloaded from ships either by hand cranes, or later steam cranes, and transferred into wagons on the quayside. It could then either be moved to storage, or into the yard for seasoning. Alternatively, the wagons could be attached to a train for transport elsewhere.

New facilities for the timber traffic were built by the SR at berth 45 where a 72,000 sq ft timber warehouse was provided as well as a storage ground. In 1930 new timber sheds were also built behind the cold store at berth 40.

Above: A picture of the then newly opened Rank's Solent Flour Mills taken from atop one of the grain conveyors from berth 103. Wagons of all of the 'Big Four' can be seen in the marshalling yard in this shot. Note the wagon in the foreground with the chalked instructions indicating its load is for the *Empress of Australia*.

(Photo: Copyright Southampton Record Office/Associated British Ports)

Principal Exports through Southampton Docks in 1927

Asbestos	Fuses (Safety)	Milk (Condensed)	Shells
Asphalt	Gloves	Nails (Copper and Iron)	Silk Goods
Blankets	Gun Powder	Nitrate	Smokers' Articles
Boots	Haberdashery	Oil	Spirits
Bullion (Gold and Silver)	Hats	Ore	Steel
Carpets	Hosiery	Paint	Tiles
Cement	Lead (Pig)	Potatoes	Tobacco (Manufactured)
Clothing	Leather Goods	Provisions	Tools
Copper	Lime	Railway Material	Wines
Cotton Goods	Linoleum	Rugs	Wire
Fish	Machinery	Sheep Dip	Woollen Goods
Fuller's Earth	Metal Goods	Shellac	Zinc Plates
Furs			

Principal Imports through Southampton Docks in 1927

Apples	Copper Matte	Machinery	Poultry (Dead)
Asbestos	Corset Materials	Maize	Preserved Fruit
Asphalt	Cotton	Matches	Preserved Meat
Bacons and Ham	Cotton Seed	Metal	Quaker Oats
Bananas	Crayfish	Mohair	Rice
Bark	Currants	Nectarines	Rubber
Barley	Dari	Oats	Seed
Beans	Dried Fruit	Offal	Silk Goods
Beer	Eggs	Oil	Skins
Bran	Earthenware	Oleo	Starch
Broccoli and Cauliflower	Flowers (Fresh)	Onions	Stationery
Buchu	Fruit (Canned)	Oranges	Stone
Buckwheat	Glass and Glassware	Ores	Strawboards
Bullion (Gold and Silver)	Grapefruit	Ostrich Feathers	Straw Envelopes
Butter	Grapes	Paper	Sugar
Cement	Health Foods	Peaches	Tobacco
Chalks	Hides	Pears	Tomatoes
Charcoal	Horns	Perfumery	Toys
Cheese	Iron and Hardware	Phosphates	Timber
Chemical Manure	Jute	Piassava	Vegetables
Chestnuts	Kainit	Pineapples	Wheat
Chilled and Frozen Meat	Lard	Plants	Wickwork
China	Leather	Plums	Wines and Spirits
Clocks	Lemons	Pollards	Wood Goods
Cocoa	Linseed	Pomegranates	Wool
Coffee	Linseed Cake	Potatoes	

Source: Southampton Docks: Handbook of Rates, Charges and General Information 1927.

On the New Docks extension a two and a half acre timber yard north-west of the carriage shed opened in 1936, operated by Montague L. Mayer Ltd. This facility included a 434ft by 127ft storage shed, which was rail connected, as well as a sawmill and offices. Montague L. Meyer is still in business today importing panel products.

Bullion

Bullion, or specie, in the form of gold, silver, precious metals, gems and other valuables has also been a long-standing cargo through the docks, both as an import and export commodity. This was transported from the 1850s in special vans equipped with safes, and later in adapted passenger luggage vans, a practice that continued into BR days.

Gold from South Africa was a significant import with £1 million of gold bullion arriving each week in 1930 which was transported to London by train, but there was also considerable transatlantic traffic. The *Southern Railway Magazine* reported that £7 million of gold bullion had been shipped on the liner *Majestic* on one trip to New York in 1934, and that the same week £11 million of bullion had been shipped on various liners.

Bananas, Fruit and Vegetables

Fruit and vegetables have also been a regular import since the earliest days of the docks, and, as noted, there was even a fruit auction house at berth 14 in the Inner Dock. Initially this traffic was from the Channel Islands and near continent. It included potatoes from Jersey, and, from the 1860s, tomatoes from Guernsey. Potatoes were traditionally transported in sacks, while the tomatoes were dispatched in wicker baskets, which had to be returned to the islands. These were later replaced by wooden trays.

Above: This close up of the postcard of Ocean Dock seen on page 9 shows a number of interesting railway related items. First in the background is a train of loaded meat wagons ready to depart to London. In the foreground is a locomotive servicing point with a water crane, and possibly coal available from the wagons on the right. Two steam locomotives can be seen, one a class B4 and the other a class C14 0-4-0 introduced on the Harbour Board lines from 1911, but which also worked in the docks. Behind the locomotives is one of the timber storage sheds.

Below: An even closer close-up of the bottom left of the postcard reveals an interesting collection of LSWR passenger luggage and 'specie' or bullion vans, both four-wheeled and bogie, including what appears to be two 44ft bogie bullion vans in the centre left, the left hand one of which has its doors open and is partially obscured by the chimney. In front of these vans, the other side of the wall, is one of the platform wagons supplied by the LSWR for internal movements of goods in the docks.

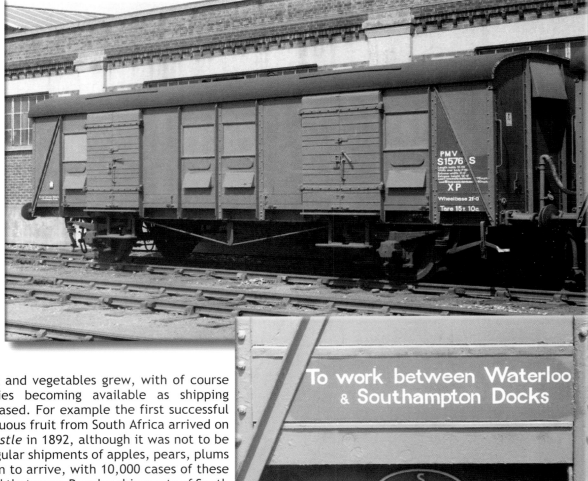

Right: Special bullion vans were in use for many years. Here on 20th May 1975 Parcels and Miscellaneous Van (PMV) No.S1576S, which was fitted with safes for bullion is seen in the Western Docks. The branding on the van can be seen bottom right along with its builder's plate.

(Photos: R. Silsbury)

The trade in fruit and vegetables grew, with of course additional varieties becoming available as shipping destinations increased. For example the first successful shipment of deciduous fruit from South Africa arrived on the *Drummond Castle* in 1892, although it was not to be until 1907 that regular shipments of apples, pears, plums and peaches began to arrive, with 10,000 cases of these fruits being landed that year. Regular shipments of South African citrus fruit started in 1910. These were often transported from the docks in insulated meat vans. A glance at the list of imports of 1927 reveals something of the extent of the variety of fruit being handled at that time.

In 1926 it was reported that between sixty and eighty thousand Guernsey tomatoes passed through the port daily at the height of the growing season. The *Southern Railway Magazine* records that on one day in 1933 2,270 wagons were used to transport the fruit traffic from the docks.

Bananas are reported to have been first landed at Southampton in 1903, and are mentioned in the Southern Railway's 1927 list of principal imports. However, a significant development in the trade came in 1931 with the inauguration of a regular service by Elders and Fyffes with over 20,000 stems being unloaded from the *Tetela* on 21st July 1931.

As can be seen from the photograph on page 73 unloading the stems was very labour intensive with each being handled individually. These were placed into covered vans that had been 'strawed', in other words a thick layer of straw was placed on the floor of the vans to cushion the bananas on their journey. Shortly afterwards a purpose-built facility was constructed at berth 25. Here deep-pocketed conveyors were used to lift the stems from the holds. These facilities were modernised in 1950s

and 60s with conveyors being used to convey the bananas directly to the trains. From the late 1960s the bananas were shipped in cartons, making handling much easier.

As the traffic grew there was the need for more specialised vehicles to convey the traffic. Therefore, the SR built special banana vans to two designs in 1935 and 1937 the first having an inside framed body and the second an outside framed. These had steam heating, and were not ventilated to aid the ripening of the bananas on their journey.

After the Second World War the first consignment of bananas arrived on 1st February 1953 with 480 wagons being required to transport them to their destinations. South African fruit traffic was also switched to berth 102 where a purpose built facility was constructed to replace the transit shed lost to enemy action. This opened in 1956, and was modernised in 1972. In addition, the Canary Fruit Terminal opened at berth 104 in 1991, while the Windward Terminal opened at berth 101 in 1993, as a result of which Southampton became the largest fruit handling port in the United Kingdom. None of these new facilities now have direct rail connections.

Right: Loading fruit could be labour intensive business as this photo demonstrates. Here Guernsey tomatoes are being loaded into a London Midland Scottish van in 1946 possibly destined for Edinburgh from the chalk markings.
(Photo: Southampton Record Office/Associated British Ports)

Left: Another labour intensive scene as bananas are manually unloaded from the Elders and Fyffes ship *Tetela* on 21st July 1931.
(Photo: Southern Railway Courtesy BRB)

Below: *Britannia* class pacific No.70004 *William Shakespeare*, without a nameplate, on a banana special from Southampton Docks at Eastleigh on 17th August 1966.
(Photo: P. Pescod Copyright Transport Treasury)

Special Cargos

In addition to the regular cargos which passed through the docks there were also special items as well, such as the hippopotamus mentioned earlier. Amongst these was the annual Christmas trade in imported turkeys, broccoli and mistletoe from France. For Christmas 1928 it was reported that 1,700 tons of turkeys, and 650 tons of mistletoe had passed through the port.

Another seasonal traffic was pigeons on their way to take part in races from the continent. In 1924 10,000 baskets of homing pigeons made their way to various parts of France from the port, while on 17th June 1925 no fewer than 2,100 baskets were dispatched to St Malo. Nine years later on 21st June 1934 special trains arrived with boxes of pigeons from Worcester, Manchester, Preston, Nottingham and elsewhere to be loaded on special sailings on the steamships *Fratton* and *Haslemere*. During the 1930s another unusual cargo was goldfish, with consignments of hundreds of thousands being imported.

Among other shipments to pass through the docks were some interesting items, such as Amelia Earhart's plane which was loaded for Le Havre in 1932 following her solo transatlantic flight. Then in January 1939 LMS Coronation class Locomotive No.6229 *Duchess of Hamilton*, masquerading as No.6220 *Coronation*, and eight *Coronation Scot* coaches were loaded for America for the New York Trade Fair. The locomotive was stranded in America until arriving back 1942, and only resuming its correct identity in 1943.

Left: One special load was the anchor chain for the liner *Homeric* seen here in the docks c.1922.
(Photo: Copyright HMRS)

Right: Many locomotives were exported via Southampton. Here the tender of a War Department oil-burning locomotive is being loaded for shipment to Suez via Port Said in 1952.
(Photo: R.K. Blencowe Collection)

Left: During the 1970s Southampton became a major centre for importing cars from Japan. On 26th February 1978 a train of cars stands ready for departure from the docks. Today Southampton Docks is a major centre for both importing and exporting cars, with the Eastern Docks being used once more for car trains.

(Photo: R. Silsbury)

Right: In January 1986 four class 59 locomotives arrived at Southampton for delivery to Foster Yeoman to haul stone trains. Here one of the locomotives is being unloaded at berth 106 on 23rd January 1986.

(Photo: R. Silsbury)

Left: A gypsum train awaits to depart from berth 109 in the Western Docks on 14th June 1999 with class 66 No.66073.

(Photo: D. Purvis)

Right: Demonstrating the twenty four hour nature of the docks operation No.66080 stands in the Western Docks in the early hours of 20th March 2008.

(Photo: D. Purvis)

Boat Trains And Other Passenger Operations

Above: The romance of the boat train is caught in this illustration of the preparations for the departure of a train from Waterloo for Southampton at the beginning of the twentieth century. Note the collecting dog for Railway Servants' Orphanage on the left.
(Commercial Postcard)

The LSWR and Ships

Although the LSWR's involvement in steamer operations is beyond the scope of this book, it was the one of the catalysts to the running of passenger services into the docks. Therefore, the early development of these services needs consideration.

One of the lesser known aspects of the LSWR was its interest from very early days in helping develop a route between London and Paris, making use of the sea-route between Southampton and Le Havre (or Havre de Grace). Already in 1830 a regular steam packet service was running twice weekly to Le Havre operated by the General Steam Packet Company, and further companies started operating on the route during the 1830s.

In that decade it was proposed to build a railway from Le Havre (literally 'the harbour') to Paris. This was eventually promoted in two sections from Paris to Rouen, and then from Rouen to Le Havre. Although the French lines were never controlled by the LSWR, the company did have a considerable involvement in their construction. Following a request for technical assistance from the promoters of the Paris to Rouen line in 1839, Joseph Locke was appointed engineer and Thomas Brassey carried out much of the construction. This was just as they had done for the London and Southampton Railway. As a result the line between Paris and Rouen was opened on 3rd May 1843 and the line from Rouen to Le Havre on 20th March 1847.

The LSWR got involved with steamer services with the formation of the South Western Steam Navigation Company in 1843. This was to link with the opening of the line between Paris and Rouen. In 1846 this was superseded by the New South Western Steam Packet Company (NSWSP), again formed by the LSWR. However, the traffic developed slowly, and so the LSWR obtained its own powers to operate steam ships, leasing the ships of the NSWSP for the purpose of its own operations. Eventually, the LSWR took over the NSWSP in July 1862.

Passenger Services and Emigration

Another key factor in the development of passenger services to and from the docks was that of emigration. In 1844 Southampton was appointed the official embarkation port for those emigrating to Canada, with the LSWR carrying emigrants 'free of charge' from London. Later in May 1845 it was reported that emigrants were conveyed directly to the quayside by the LSWR trains.

These are the earliest recorded passenger workings into the docks, and must have been to the north side of the Outer Dock, then the only facility in the docks. Whether these trains were locomotive worked into the docks or hauled by horses is unclear, although the former is possible, as LSWR locomotives could work into the docks by this time.

The emigration traffic developed with sailings to Australia

commencing in August 1852, with emigrants being transported from Waterloo by train. By October that year Southampton had been designated by the Government as its official emigration port, part of the reason being that trains could be run directly to the 'ship's side'. Forty emigrant ships are recorded as departing the port the following year.

Emigration continued to play a significant role in the life of the port into the twentieth century. Readers of *Southern Rails Around Southampton* will have already heard of the Atlantic Park Hostel, which was established in the 1920s by the shipping lines at the site of what would later be Southampton airport. This had its own halt to permit migrants to board trains for the docks. Even post the Second World War and into the 1970s, there was still substantial emigration to Australia, although as with other passenger traffic, increasingly those travelling arrived by road rather than rail.

Boat Trains

It is uncertain when the first boat trains ran in connection with the Southampton to Le Havre steamer service. However, the LSWR minutes in 1847 talk about considering the option of 'direct communication' to Paris, and giving permission for steps to be taken to carry this out. Therefore advertisements in the *Hampshire Advertiser* for the NSWSP in 1848, offered through tickets between London and Paris at a cost of 48 shillings (£2.40) first class and 36 shillings (£1.80) second class. Although no specific train times were stated in the advertisement, they did say that the sailing vessels would await the arrival of 'the trains from London'.

Whether this meant the trains were run into the docks is not said, but given that other passenger trains had done so by this time it seems likely. Certainly another newspaper article of December 1851, states that railway carriages were run into the docks for the benefit of passengers from France travelling to the Great Exhibition.

Passenger numbers were increasing, on 23rd June 1856 it was said that 1,100 passengers had landed at the port the previous week, with 3,500 items of baggage. By 1868 the LSWR timetable advertised that passengers for Paris could travel on the 9.00 pm service from Waterloo on Mondays, Wednesdays and Fridays, and be conveyed into Southampton Docks alongside the steamers while remaining in their railway carriages. This had increased to a daily service by 1883.

Up until this point the only regular train services that seem to have been run into the docks were in connection with the French and Channel Islands services, and made use of standard LSWR carriages, although there were requests for 'special trains' from operators such as P&O as far back as the 1840s. However, with the takeover of the docks by the LSWR in 1892, and the arrival of American Line's transatlantic services in the port, the LSWR decided to build ten bogie first class carriages for American Line's boat trains.

These were sumptuously finished at a cost of £1,190 each, and became known as the *American Eagle* or simply *Eagle* stock. They were the first LSWR coaches with semi-elliptical roofs giving extra headroom inside the carriages. Six bogie brake vans were ordered in 1893 to complement the *Eagle* stock, and a second set of ten *Eagle* carriages was built in 1894.

To haul these 'flagship' services the LSWR as well as its successors the SR and BR of course employed their latest express locomotives. Therefore, through the years the boat trains were hauled by 4-4-0s such as the Drummond C8s and T9s, while later it would be 4-6-0s such as the T14s and the Urie *King Arthurs* or his H15s. From the late 1920s Maunsell *Lord Nelsons* would be employed, and later the Bulleid *Merchant Navy*, *West Country* and *Battle of Britain* pacifics were used, finally supplemented by BR standard classes.

In the early 1900s there were regular daily trains run in connection with the steamer services to France and the

Left: A '330' class 0-6-0 saddle tank No.334 waits for a boat train, hauled by an unidentified LSWR 4-4-0, to pass between the warehouses at berths 34 and 35 in the Old Docks in the early years of the twentieth century.
(Photographer Unknown Courtesy *The Railway Magazine*)

Channel Islands, and trains run to connect with liners on a regular schedule, as well as others which ran on an 'as needed' basis. The timing and number of the latter depended on the arrival and sailing times of the steamer, or the number of passengers embarking or leaving the ship.

By the summer of 1914, just before the outbreak of World War One, there were trains in connection with the steamers to Le Havre and the Channel Islands at 9.50 pm (June only), or 10.30 pm (July, August and September) Monday to Saturdays, the latter being a supper-train, while on Saturdays there was a extra train at 9.30 am to connect with a daytime sailing. There was also a through service from the GWR with connections from Liverpool and Manchester via Reading and Basingstoke to link with

the Le Havre boat.

Boat trains ran in connection with the Cherbourg ferries from Waterloo at 8.15 pm on Tuesdays, Thursdays and Saturdays. Trains for the St Malo ferry ran from Waterloo on the same days in June, increasing to every weekday in the summer peak, but the timings of these trains varied daily between early afternoon and evening.

For the trains which ran in connection with ships bound for further flung destinations the situation was more complex. Some of these sailings ran on a regular or semi-regular basis, and for these services the connecting boat trains in summer 1914 are summarised in the table below:

Table of Boat Trains regularly departing from Waterloo for Southampton Docks Summer 1914
(More than one train could be run where necessary)

Day	Departure Times	Shipping Line	Destination	Frequency
Monday	9.30 am	Norddeutscher Lloyd	Sydney	Every 28 days
Tuesday	9.30 am 10.15 am 10.15 am	Norddeutscher Lloyd Nederland Royal Mail Rotterdam Lloyd	Far East/Japan Far East Colombo	Alternate weeks Alternate weeks Alternate weeks
Wednesday	8.30 am (2nd & 3rd class) 9.30 am (2nd class) 9.30 am 9.30 am 9.45 am (1st class)	White Star American Norddeutscher Lloyd Royal Mail White Star	New York New York New York Jamaica/New York New York	Weekly Weekly Weekly Alternate weeks Weekly
Thursday	10.05 am	Union Castle	South Africa	Monthly
Friday	9.30 am	Royal Mail	Brazil/River Plate	Weekly
Saturday	8.55 am (3rd class) 10.00 am (2nd class) 10.00 am (3rd class) 10.00 am (1st & 2nd class) 11.35 am (1st & 2nd class)	American American Union Castle Union Castle Union Castle	New York New York South Africa Intermediate(slow) South Africa Intermediate(slow) South Africa (Mail)	Weekly Weekly Weekly Weekly Weekly

Left: The old Continental Booking Office inside Gate No.5 at the Old Docks.
(Photo: Southern Railway Courtesy BRB)

Right: The scene as an *Ocean Liner Express* arrives with passengers for the *Queen Elizabeth* on 18th March 1949. Ocean Terminal was not completed by this time, so this photo was probably taken at berth 46 or 47. Passengers have vacated the *Pullman* carriage *Zena* for checking in. *Zena* was built in 1928 originally for service on the GWR, it has now been preserved and is part of the *Venice Simplon Orient Express* fleet.
(Photo: Southampton Record Office/Associated British Ports)

There were other services that ran more irregularly as sailing times varied. These included trains in connection with Cunard Line's services to Canada. Other trains ran as required to serve the Deutsche Ost Afrika Line services to Cape Town, and Beira, both of which ran twice a month with trains departing Waterloo at 9.25 am on weekdays and 10.05 am on Sundays depending on the day the boats sailed. Similarly the Hamburg-America's services to New York, Boston, Cuba and Rio de Janeiro were served by trains which ran as required. The Norddeutscher Lloyd line also had an 'intermediate' service to New York. All of which made life somewhat complex for the LSWR's timetablers.

Where there was more than one train connecting with a sailing, particularly in the case of transatlantic departures, then the second and third class passengers would be conveyed to Southampton first. This was partly due to their larger numbers and also to allow for health checks to be carried out, as anyone showing signs of ailment or illness would be refused entry at New York, and would have to be brought back at the company's expense. It also meant that the first class passengers could enjoy a later start to their journeys, and would be whisked from the train to their cabins on arrival at the docks. In the year of writing, 2012, the White Star departure times are of particular interest as they would bear relationship to the departure of the trains for the *Titanic* on Wednesday 10th April 1912.

Boat Trains and the Southern

With the outbreak of World War One cross-channel services were severely curtailed, especially as a significant number of steamers were requisitioned by the

Admiralty. It is not unreasonable, therefore, to suggest that the numbers of boat trains followed suit.

After World War One the liner traffic gradually began to resume. During 1922 165,205 passengers landed at and 190,905 set sail from Southampton. Passenger traffic began to increase significantly after the Grouping, and with it the number of boat trains.

The *Southern Railway Magazine* recorded that between 7.00 am on Friday 3rd April 1925 and 9.00 am on Saturday 4th, eight liners arrived at the port and ten departed. In connection with these fifteen special boat trains had been run from Waterloo. Similarly six trains to Waterloo were run in conjunction with the arrival of the *Leviathan* and *Majestic* on 19th June 1925, three in connection with each. Handling times could also be impressive. When the *Majestic* docked at 1.26 pm on 18th September 1925, the first train carrying first class passengers left at 2.21 pm, reaching Waterloo at 4.10 pm.

By 1927 there were twelve timetabled paths available for boat trains to the docks to run as required between 6.00 am and 12.00 noon Monday to Friday, with approximately one path an hour available up until 9.00 pm. At 9.00 pm the cross-channel train would depart Waterloo arriving at the Channel Islands shed in the docks at 10.49 pm, with an extra path available at 9.50 pm if required. In March 1928 there were no fewer than 45 scheduled boat trains run for the liners.

A significant change occurred in January 1931 when *Pullman* cars were introduced on what were now referred to as the *Ocean Liner Expresses*. It was reported that 50% of first class passengers on these trains now travelled by

Above: In April 1938 class H15 4-6-0 No.523 passes Byfleet with a Southampton Docks to Waterloo boat train.
(Photo: C.R.L. Coles Copyright RailPhotoprints-Dave Cobbe Collection)

Pullman. However, it was not all good news as the depression of the early 1930s led to a significant reduction in traffic. Slowly trade began to recover, and on Saturday 8th September 1934 26 special boat trains departed from the docks for Waterloo.

Of course at this point the New Docks had come into use, but at this time the only connection to the new berths was via the Old Docks and the Harbour Board lines. Trains on these lines were in the charge of a docks department shunter, who travelled with them throughout their journey from Canute Road to the New Docks or vice versa.

At this time too, the concept of cruising began to take off. In 1927 40 cruises departed from Southampton, increasing to 60 in 1936, and 85 the following year. These were not, of course, necessarily on a regular schedule, and so provided another timetabling challenge for the provision of boat trains. The rise in passenger numbers continued and in 1937 some 301,000 people embarked at Southampton, and 321,000 disembarked, the vast majority of whom would have arrived or departed by train.

Flying Boat Services

An interesting variation on the boat trains were those trains that ran in connection with Imperial Airways' Flying Boat Service in the late 1930s. On 16th January 1937 passengers were brought to Southampton from Waterloo in a special *Pullman* car, with an attached brake van, that

had been coupled to the rear of the 8.30 am service from Waterloo. At Southampton Central these carriages were detached and run to berth 50 in the Old Docks, which was the terminal used for tenders taking passengers out to liners berthed in the Solent. In this case passengers were transferred to the flying boat station at Hythe, for the flight to Alexandria by the flying boat *Centaurus*.

Originally these trains served the twice weekly departures to India and Australia as well as the inbound services from Africa, which also arrived twice a week. One or more *Pullmans* would be used, and during the journey from Waterloo the flight clerk had to weigh the passengers and baggage prior to the train's arrival in the docks. Later in June 1937 outbound services to South Africa started from Southampton, and trains provided as required.

By 1938 the flying boat services departed to South Africa on Tuesdays and Saturdays, Africa on Fridays, and India, the Far East and Brisbane on Thursdays and Sundays. At this point the connecting train service ran the previous evening, with passengers being accommodated at the South Western Hotel overnight before being taken across to Hythe for their flights. Subsequently air operations were transferred to berth 108, where land was rented from the SR in March 1938 for £500 per annum, and here a wooden terminal building and jetty were constructed.

Another change to these trains came when a dedicated

Above: Inaugural *Imperial Airways Special* from London Victoria platform 17 on 6th June 1939 with class T9 4-4-0 No.338 in charge.
(Photo: Stevenson Copyright Getty Images Hulton Archive Ref.57066785)

terminal was opened at the headquarters of Imperial Airways in London, which connected through to platform 17 at Victoria station. From here on 6th June 1939 at 8.05 pm the *Imperial Airways Special*, headed by T9 class 4-4-0 No.338, departed for Southampton to connect with the flying boat service. Passengers again staying overnight at the South Western Hotel before their early morning departure from berth 108. In the reverse direction passengers were conveyed directly back to London departing at 1.23 pm. These trains were booked to run daily except Mondays and Saturdays, but due to the outbreak of World War Two they did not last long.

After the war British Overseas Airways Corporation (BOAC) had taken over the services, and opened a dedicated terminal at berth 50 on 14th April 1948. Flights now operated daily to Australia, South Africa, Pakistan, and Japan. Aquila Airways also began operations in 1949, continuing until 1958, BOAC having pulled out in 1950. However, it is not clear if special trains operated in connection with these flights, although there were rail facilities at the terminal.

Troop Trains

As has been mentioned previously a significant traffic through the port was troops heading out to foreign postings or returning home. This continued annually, but increased dramatically during times of war. During the

Crimean War in the 1850s 90,000 men passed through the port, being transported by P&O ships to their destinations.

The Boer War also put a huge strain on the rail infrastructure, for example, it was reported that on 20th October 1899 five transports left the docks for South Africa. Readers of *Southern Rails Around Southampton* will also have heard of the accident at the Docks station on 30th October 1899, which was partly attributed to the signalman's fatigue due to the number of troop trains that had passed through that day.

Of course the two World Wars were the major periods of troop movements through the docks. During the First World War it is estimated that some seven million soldiers and 3.38 million tons of stores were transported via the port. This included a significant number of casualties, which will be discussed later.

Although the port was closed for much of the Second World War there were two periods when substantial numbers of troops passed through the docks in a short period. The first was at the commencement of hostilities when, between September 1939 and June 1940, some 800,000 troops along with 375,765 tons of equipment and stores for the British Expeditionary Force, were shipped via Southampton to France.

The second period was the run-up and aftermath to D-Day

Left: On 17th May 1953 the Railway Correspondence and Travel Society (RCTS) ran an excursion from Eastleigh to Fawley and then into the docks. Here the tour is seen at the rail terminal at berth 50 used for the flying boat services with *USA* tank No.30062 at the head. It is uncertain how much this terminal was used for passenger services, particularly after BOAC ceased operation, but the author has seen at least two photographs of trains at the terminal, but unfortunately has not been able to get copies for publication.
This photo was taken from one of the pontoons at the flying boat terminal.
(Photo: G.F. Bloxam
Copyright P.F. Bloxam)

in June 1944, when huge numbers of troops had to be moved into the port in a very short time span, both before and after the event. Some idea of the scale of the operation can be seen in the figures that in total throughout the war over 4.3 million soldiers passed through the port. No fewer than 3.5 million of these were between D-Day and the end of the war.

Excursions

Another significant source of passenger traffic into the docks, only this time not to sail from the port, was the excursion days that were offered by the SR. The first one was held on Thursday 18th August 1927, when trains had

been organised and special fares of 5s 9d (28p) offered from London for the opportunity to look round the docks and board some of the liners. However, the night before this it looked like it might be a quiet day as only 300 had booked. In the event 3,280 people travelled down in six special trains, the first of which arrived at 12.31pm at berth 43.

The excursions were repeated on 12th September and 17th October that year, and then became a regular feature, with 70,000 visitors coming to the port in 1928. It was not only excursions that toured the docks, but also private parties were catered for, which could number between a dozen and two thousand. In addition large

Left: Of course troop trains operated to many parts of the country, here is a cosmopolitan scene with ex-LMS *Patriot* No. 45516 *The Bedfordshire and Hertfordshire Regiment*, still in LMS livery, about to depart from the New Docks with a train of ex-LNER Gresley coaches in February 1950.
(Photo: S.C. Townroe Copyright R.K. Blencowe)

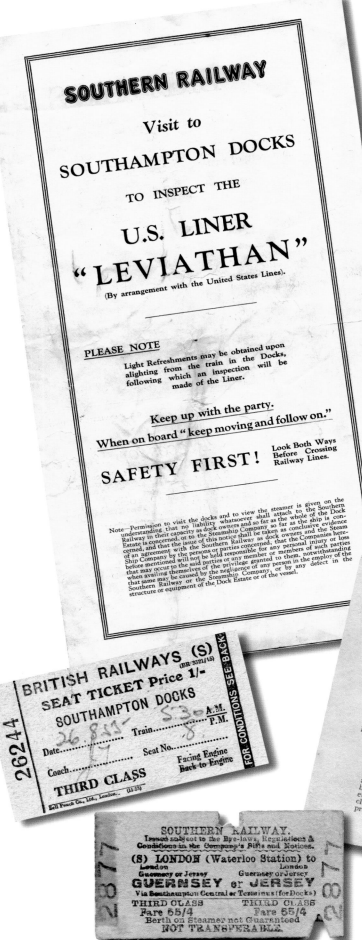

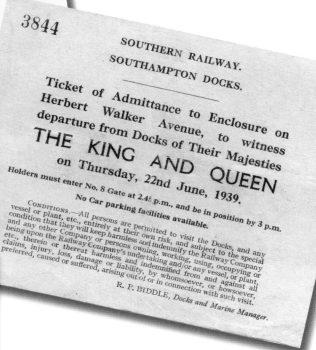

numbers of school outings also frequented the docks, and in October 1936 the SR Docks Committee minutes noted that 24,000 school children and teachers had visited the port on 56 special trains so far that year.

Special Events

There were also those visiting the docks for special events, such as in connection with a naval review. For Queen Victoria's Diamond Jubilee Naval Review in 1897 29 trains ran to the docks as well as extra trains to the Southampton stations. In fact so great were the number of trains that Canute Road, Chapel Road, Bevois Street, Mount Pleasant and Dukes Road crossings were closed to road traffic for the occasion.

During the days of the Southern 32 special trains were run to the docks for the Silver Jubilee Naval Review on 16th July 1935. The Coronation Naval Review on Thursday 20th May 1937 attracted even larger numbers with no fewer than 88 special trains operating between London and the docks. In the meantime, the arrival of the Queen Mary on 27th March 1936 also provoked a lot of interest, with 18 special trains conveying 6,984 sightseers arriving from London, Birmingham, Bristol, Leicester, Bedford, Dover, Brighton and South Wales on Sunday 29th March to observe the liner in the docks.

Above: Sporting its BR number of No.30779 but still with *Southern* emblazoned on its tender *King Arthur* class *Sir Colgrevance* departs from the Old Docks through Gate No.3 on 17th March 1949. The post-nationalisation time-frame is confirmed by the presence of two ex-GWR *Siphon* vehicles in the train. (Photo: Southampton Record Office/Associated British Ports)

Above: On 4th October 1949 *Lord Nelson* class No.30857 (although at this time it still carried its SR number No.857) *Lord Howe* rounds the curve in from Millbrook through Gate No.12 with a boat train for the *Aquitania*. In the left background is the Toogoods building, and the Millbrook goods shed, while on the right is the General Motors factory that was badly damaged during World War Two. (Photo: Southampton Record Office/Associated British Ports)

Post War

After the war traffic slowly resumed. The first Channel Islands boat train departed Waterloo at 5.55 pm on 25th June 1945. By October 1947 it was again operating three times a week with a 9 pm departure, the train for the incoming ferry having departed from Southampton at 5.20 pm. However, operations to Le Havre did not recommence until 13th January 1947, and to St Malo from 14th July 1947. Even then the St Malo service seems to have been summer only, and the Le Havre service only operated on Mondays during the winter of 1947.

Other shipping services gradually resumed, the *Queen Elizabeth* made its first transatlantic crossing from Southampton after the war on 16th October 1946. This was its first 'civilian' voyage, the ship having been requisitioned immediately on its completion at the beginning of the war. Later the refitted *Queen Mary* departed on her first post-war trip to New York on 31st July 1947. Other liners and routes also gradually resumed business.

British Railways

After nationalisation, British Railways continued to operate the boat trains in connection with both the ferries and liners. The opening of Ocean Terminal in July 1950 provided a 'state of the art' facility for handing the liner traffic, with rail facilities well catered for.

One major event in the early 1950s was the Spithead Naval Review in connection with the Coronation in June 1953. On this occasion 42 trains ran from Waterloo to the docks during the period 13th to 16th June, with 31 being dispatched from the docks over a four hour period at the conclusion of proceedings on the 16th.

Up until this point the boat trains had been unnamed going under the generic terms of *Continental Expresses* or *Ocean Liner Expresses*. In 1952 this changed. First of all the entry of a new ship, the SS *Normannia*, on to the Le Havre route caused the naming of the connecting boat train from Waterloo. This became known as the *Normandy Express* from 30th June 1952.

Next came *The Cunarder*, the first of which ran on 2nd July 1952, departing Waterloo at 7.05pm with *Merchant Navy* No.35004 *Cunard White Star* in charge, serving first class passengers for the *Queen Mary* and *Queen Elizabeth*. After this on 8th July 1952 came the *Statesman*. This was an all-*Pullman* train and first run in connection with the maiden voyage of the SS *United States*.

Other services followed, from 1953 the *Union Castle Express* operated in connection with its Thursday sailings to South Africa, along with the *Holland-American* and *The South American*. The latter operated in connection with the Royal Mail Lines' sailings. In 1954 the train operated in connection with the St Malo sailings became the *Brittany Express*, while the *Greek Line* express was also introduced. The following year the *Arosa Line* services started running.

There were later additions such as the *Springbok* for the Union Castle South African sailings, and the *Sitmar Line* in 1960. Some were introduced in connection with *P&O Cruises*. Locomotive headboards and carriage roof boards

Above: *Battle of Britain* class No.34081 *92 Squadron*, now preserved at the Nene Valley Railway, departs from Ocean Terminal in 1959 bound for Waterloo.
(Photo: Copyright Colour-Rail 340577)

Above: On 18th June 1955 *King Arthur* class No.30748 *Vivien* departs from the Old Docks with a boat train from the Continental Transit Shed at the Outer Dock heading towards Gate No.5.
(Photo: Peter T. Hay)

Above: *Lord Nelson* class No.30859 *Lord Hood* departs from the Old Docks on 26th June 1957 with empty stock heading towards Gate No.3. The headcode is interestingly for Southampton Docks to Waterloo via East Putney.
(Photo: R.C. Riley Copyright Transport Treasury)

Left: In July 1957 *Lord Nelson* class No.30854 *Howard of Effingham* stands at the Continental Transit Shed with the *Brittany Express*. The corner of the Continental Booking Office can be seen on the right.
(Photo: Copyright R.K. Blencowe Collection)

Above: *USA* class No.30070 shunts at the Continental Transit Shed on 18th June 1955. The collection of classic cars is worth noting, as is the Continental Booking Office in the background. No.30070 was transferred to Ashford works in 1963 having been renumbered DS238 and named *Wainwright*, lasting in service until September 1967. It was preserved at the Kent and East Sussex Railway, where it is still based today.
(Photo: Peter T. Hay)

Left: The former Continental Booking Hall in March 2011.

were provided. The latter were also produced for untitled trains such as for British India Lines services.

These trains were underwritten by the shipping companies, which guaranteed a minimum number of passengers for any given train. *Pullmans* were provided for these services under the jurisdiction of the Pullman Car Company. These were added to trains on an 'as required' basis depending on how many tickets had been sold for the journey. This led to much shunting and re-marshalling of sets, which was very inefficient.

The early to mid-fifties could be seen as very much the height of the liner traffic and also of the boat trains. Passenger numbers at Southampton reached a peak in 1955, most of these would still have been passing through the gates by train. However, the combination of air travel and road transportation led to the decline of both the transatlantic trade, and also the boat trains respectively. In 1956 there were up to 28 timetabled paths on Mondays

to Fridays to be used as required for the liner expresses from Waterloo to the docks taking between 96 to 110 minutes for the journey. In addition the two ferry expresses were timetabled at 6.35 pm from Waterloo for the *Brittany Express* and 9.00 pm for the *Normandy Express*. There were also up to four extra timetabled paths on Fridays for the ferry traffic. These trains served both the cross-channel and Channel Islands traffic.

By the last pre-electrification timetable in 1967 the number of services had reduced dramatically. The Channel Islands and cross-channel trains had disappeared completely, with the transfer of those ferry operations to Weymouth in 1961 and 1964 respectively. Only a maximum of eight timetabled paths from Waterloo to the docks on weekdays for the liner trains remained. With electrification the number of trains diminished, and were now no longer named or with *Pullmans,* which had been withdrawn in 1963. This was as the numbers of sailings decreased, and the number of passengers arriving and

Left: No.34065 *Hurricane* approaches Ocean Terminal with an unnamed boat train on 26th April 1962.
(Photo: Colin Hogg Copyright Bluebell Railway Museum Archive)

Right: On 29th May 1992 class 33 No.33102 and 4-TC units Nos. 410 and 417 await to depart empty to Eastleigh from berths 105/6 in the Western Docks. They had previously arrived with passengers for the P&O liner *Canberra*. No.33102 has been preserved and is currently based on the Swanage Railway.
(Photographer Unknown)

departing from the port by road increased.

Privatisation

Despite this some boat trains continued to run. In August 1972 there were still 31 timetabled boat trains, or *Ocean Liner Trains* as they were advertised, from Waterloo. But through the late 1970s and into the 1980s the number of trains continued to fall. However, in the 1990s with privatisation, things went back to the past when the *Venice-Simplon Orient Express British Pullman* started to run from London in connection with Cunard sailings. The *British Pullman* is composed of *Pullman* cars which have been preserved from the 'glory days' of the *Pullman*

expresses. These trains even employed steam power in the mid-1990s, but today are less frequent.

Bath Travel began to run services from Scotland and Northern England to the docks in 2008 using the *Blue Pullman* train for cruise passengers under the brand name of *Cruise Savers*. Their services still continue to operate two or three times a month, and more recently another operator, Barrhead Travel, has begun to run trains from Scotland. These services generally use the facilities at the Queen Elizabeth II terminal, as the platform in the Western Docks is very short. However, the increasing number of car transporter trains using the Eastern Docks will probably limit the capacity to increase these services.

Right: Steam returns for *The Cunarder* on 15th October 1995 when *Merchant Navy* pacific No.35028 *Clan Line* prepares to double-head the 18.30 departure from Queen Elizabeth II cruise terminal to London Victoria with class 47 No.47725.

(Photo: D. Purvis)

Left: Class 67 No.67006 *Royal Sovereign* at the Queen Elizabeth II terminal platform on 27th October 2012 with the 10.05 am departure for Glasgow Central operated on behalf of Barrhead Travel.

(Photo: D. Purvis)

Above: Excursions and tours have always played a part in the passenger operations at the docks from the 1840s. Here the RCTS railtour of the Fawley branch and docks has reached Ocean Terminal with No.30062 still in charge on 17th May 1953. The rolling stock certainly looks an interesting set of pre-Grouping stock. (Photo: G.F. Bloxam Copyright P.F. Bloxam)

Above: Another railtour enters the docks as 4-6-0 BR standard class 4 No.75070 crosses Canute Road with watching admirers on 20th March 1966. It is in charge of the RCTS *The Solent* railtour which has travelled on this leg from Salisbury and is now heading for Ocean Terminal. Car aficionados will recognise the distinctive designs of the Ford Zephyr and Ford Cortina in the picture. (Photo: John H. Bird Copyright Southern-Images)

Above: *West Country* No.34012 *Lapford* passes Vauxhall on 11th May 1967 with the down *Cunarder*.　　　　(Photo: P.F. Bloxam)

Above: *Battle of Britain* class No.34053 *Sir Keith Park* heads the down *Union Castle Express* near Litchfield tunnel on 1st April 1965. The headcode is for Waterloo to Western Docks via Millbrook.　　　　(Photo: P. Pescod Copyright Transport Treasury)

Above: *West Country* No.34018 *Axminster* heads through Eastleigh with one of the first *Statesman* boat trains in 1952.
(Photo: Copyright Colour-Rail 340123)

Above: Another named boat train, this time the *Holland-American*, with *West Country* No.34005 *Barnstaple* in charge at Shawford in 1954 heading for the docks.
(Photo: B.J. Swain Copyright Colour-Rail BRS420)

Above: *West Country* No. 34009 *Lyme Regis* prepares to cross Canute Road past Terminus station with a *Greek Line* boat train in September 1963.
(Photo: A. Sainty Collection Copyright Colour-Rail BRS1043)

Above: The Royal Mail Line's *The South American* heads for the Eastern Docks, probably in the mid-1950s judging from the early BR emblem on *King Arthur* class No.30779 *Sir Colgrevance's* tender and the Maunsell brake-end coach on set 353, much of which is composed of Bulleid stock in crimson and cream livery with possibly two *Pullmans* in the formation. Later of course, BR Mark One stock would supercede the Bulleid and Maunsell coaches.
(Photographer Unknown Copyright Southern-Images)

Above: Of course not all boat trains were glamorous titled expresses. Here Standard class 4 2-6-4 tank locomotive No.80139 approaches Southampton Junction off the curve from Southampton Central, with a train which has been detached at Central from the 1.20 pm from Waterloo on 23rd March 1967 and is now heading for the docks.   (Photo: John H. Bird Copyright Southern-Images)

Above: *West Country* pacific No.34025 *Whimple* departs from the Old Docks through Gate No.3 and past the now-closed Terminus station on 13th June 1967 with a boat train with passengers from the *Queen Elizabeth*. This would be among the last steam worked boat trains before the end of steam on Southern Region.
(Photo: John H. Bird Copyright Southern-Images)

Operating the Docks Lines in the 1950s

Above: BR standard class 5 mixed-traffic locomotive No.73093, built at Derby in 1955, leaving the Eastern Docks with a boat train on 29th March 1967 passing the shunters' cabin, where several shunters appear to be taking a break.

(Photo: Copyright Colour-Rail 381350)

The mid to late 1950s can be said to be the heyday of the docks railways with the transatlantic liner service at its peak. Road transport was yet to make substantial inroads on the amount of goods and passengers arriving at and departing from the docks by rail. Therefore, one question is how were over 70 miles of track, and nearly one thousand hand-levered points, operated with no signals save at the crossing of Canute Road?

Clearly from what we have seen the amount and variety of trains passing over the docks lines was considerable, from main line expresses to mixed goods trains, presenting a significant logistical challenge for those responsible for the docks lines. One insight into the way these trains were dealt with is given by the *Special Instructions relative to the Working Of Traffic into and out of Southampton Docks and over the Dock Lines*, issued by the British Transport Commission to its employees at the docks, the edition used being dated 1958. This was of course an updating of the instructions issued to employees under the LSWR and SR previously.

At the heart of railway operations on the docks was the Traffic Controller, who had a staff of over one hundred in the mid-1950s. It was his office that took the strategic decisions on operations, based on the list of arrivals and departures of shipping, the natures of cargoes, and their destination etc.. Where shipping services were on a regular schedule then this made things easier, but still

there were variables to be taken into account, such as passenger numbers and types of cargo. For the more irregular sailings and occasional, or 'one-off', events things had to be more flexible. There were of course other circumstances to be dealt with such as delays to shipping arrivals.

In charge of the shunting operations was the Chief Freight Inspector, whose permission was needed for any movements into or out of the docks. There were also Yard Inspectors or foremen responsible for the various shunting yards in both the Old and New Docks. Within the docks the shunters were responsible for all movements including passenger and freight trains, shunting movements and light engine running. They were also to ensure the protection of road and foot traffic when trains crossed the public roads.

There were key priorities in the operation of trains, the first was the passage of passenger trains, with 'every endeavour made to give same a clear run', according to the rule book. Having brought their trains into the docks, the shunters were then responsible to see that the main line locomotive was released as soon as possible, and dispatched from the docks estate. The next priorities to be dealt with were the arrival and departure of freight workings, followed by shunting and light engine movements.

Left: A tight squeeze for *West Country* pacific No.34004 *Yeovil* through Gate No.5 as it departs from the Old Docks with a St Malo boat train on 25th June 1964. The National Provincial Bank building is on the left. (Photo: Bert Moody)

Left: Nine years previously, but on the same working, No.258, *King Arthur* class No.30748 *Vivien* departs from the Old Docks across Canute Road on 18th June 1955. Note the flagman with both flag and bell supervising the crossing as per the operating instructions. No.30748 would last in service until September 1957.

(Photo: Peter T. Hay)

Left: A similar view to that above on 23rd August 2012.

Right: The remains of Gate No.6 on the same day.

Movements into and out of the Old Docks

Trains entering the Old Docks from the Terminus would access the estate via Gates No.3 or No.5. Gate No.5 gave access to the Front Yard, as well as the Channel Islands and Continental berths. Meanwhile, Gate No.3 was used for all other areas of the Old Docks, as well as for the Harbour Board lines, and the link to the New Docks.

When a train was required to enter the docks, the pointsman at Canute Road ground frame would advise the Inspector, or if he was not available, the person in charge at the Empress Dock Yard, and request permission for the movement to take place. The Inspector would then give the details of the movement to the duty shunter, who would then proceed to the appropriate gate to take charge of the train immediately it entered the docks.

In addition, the Canute Road pointsman would sound a bell at either Ocean Terminal or the Empress Docks Inspectors' cabin, as a warning of the impending movement and notify staff of its destination. The table below gives the variety of bell-codes used, which would have to be acknowledged. A similar system was used for the pointsman to notify the gateman on duty, the gateman responding when the shunter was ready to receive the train. Having signalled the train, the pointsman was also supposed to assist in helping control road traffic as the train passed over Canute Road, unless a flagman was on duty.

Freight trains were directed into reception roads where the wagonmarker would record the details of each wagon and then mark them for the appropriate unloading point. Trains would then be shunted so that wagons could be sent to their destinations. Loading or unloading was the responsibility of the sheetmen and ropemen. Loaded wagons were collected from their loading points and brought to a marshalling yard to be made up into trains, the details of each loaded wagon being taken by a

Bell Code Between Canute Road Ground Frame and Ocean Terminal

Description of Train and Destination	No. of Rings
Train for Ocean Terminal about to pass Canute Road Ground Frame.	1 long

Bell Code Between Canute Road Ground Frame and Empress Dock

Description of Train and Destination	No. of Rings
Train or engine via Empress Dock	1 long
Train or engine via Central Road to Chalk Roads or 46/47 sheds	2 long
Train or engine for New Docks via Harbour Board Lines	3 short
Train or engine for Dock East (Gate No.3)	4 short
Train or engine for 50 berth via Gate No.3	5 short

Right: Loco and shunting crew of ex-LBSCR class E1 No.32689 pose for the camera by Central Road in the Old Docks on 26th June 1957.
(Photo: R.C. Riley Copyright Transport Treasury)

numbertaker.

The information gathered by the wagonmarkers and numbertakers were then passed to the Traffic Controller's Freight Rolling Stock Section, where it was collated. From this was produced the *Daily Freight Rolling Stock Return*, which accounted for every wagon on the docks estate. Using this information the Traffic Controller's office liaised with the District Traffic Superintendent at Southampton Central, who would arrange for the supply of additional wagons, or the removal of those surplus to requirements as needed.

When passenger trains were leaving the docks the Passenger Inspector would advise the Freight Inspector, as well as the pointsman at Canute Road, of the departure point and approximate time of the train, so that they could prepare for its movement. Again the pointsman would advise the gatemen by bell code, which would be acknowledged when the gates had been opened. After this the pointsman would clear the signals, or, in the case of Gate No.5, ask the signalman at Southampton Yard box to clear the appropriate signal. Freight trains would be advised to the Canute Road pointsman by either the Freight Inspector, or person in charge at Empress Yard, while light engines could be notified by the shunter in charge.

Movements on the Harbour Board Lines

For movements of trains between Terminus and Town Quay or the New Docks, the lines via Gates Nos. 1 and 3 were used. For trains going from the Old Docks to the New Docks, the Inspector would notify the pointsman at Canute Road, the foreman at the Town Quay, the Inspector in charge at the New Docks, and the gatemen involved. If the movement was a passenger train then additionally the Inspector had to inform the stationmaster at Terminus. He in turn would arrange for all the facing points along the route to be 'plugged', so that they could not move under the passage of the train. For all trains, or light engines, travelling between the docks the stationmaster would also provide handsignalmen at the road crossings, and a docks shunter

Left: *USA* class No.30073 enters the New Docks with a transfer train of RCH containers on 26th April 1962. The shunter is riding on the cab steps. No.30073 lasted in service until 1966 when it was withdrawn and scrapped.
(Photo: Colin Hogg Courtesy Bluebell Railway Museum Archive)

Right: Wagon destinations were often chalked onto the sides of wagons by the wagonmarkers. On 26th April 1962 class E2 No.32104 with a 12 ton van, which has had various notes scrawled on it, shunting by Central Road in the Old Docks.
(Photo: Colin Hogg Courtesy Bluebell Railway Museum Archive)

would ride with all trains throughout their journey. Similar arrangements applied for trains traversing the line in the reverse direction.

If the movement was to or from Town Quay then the foreman at the quay, the Freight Inspector, the gateman at Gate No.1 and the pointsman at Canute Road, had to liaise before any train or engine could proceed to or from the Quay. In addition the speed restriction of 5mph still applied to all movements along the Harbour Board lines, and 3mph when crossing Canute Road, as opposed to the 10mph limit on the rest of the docks lines.

Movements into or out of the New Docks via Millbrook

As in the Old Docks shunters had to travel with any movement within the New Docks, which also had its own Inspector. The rule book stated that when a train was approaching Southampton Central the signalman at Millbrook was to telephone the Docks shunter, and again when it was approaching Millbrook. In the meantime the shunter was to go to Gate No.12 and open the gates, after which he was to advise the signalman at Millbrook he was ready to accept the train.

The signalman would then release the frame so that the shunter could operate the signals. After the train had passed the Home signal the shunter would replace it to danger, and then join the engine. For departures the Inspector would inform the Docks shunter the approximate time the train was due to leave. The train would then proceed with the shunter to the up Home signal at Gate No.12. There the shunter would advise the signalman at Millbrook that the train was ready to depart. If he was able to accept the train the signalman would release the frame, so the shunter could operate the signals, and the train could leave the docks.

Communications

In all this communication and liaison was a key factor. The LSWR had provided a telephone system in the docks in the 1890s. This system had been improved by the SR and extended to the New Docks when they came into use. However, in 1955 radio-telephones were fitted in the cabs of locomotives. But interestingly the *Special Instructions* of 1958 make no mention of these 'new-fangled' devices. In later times of course, radio communication was increasingly used, transforming many of the operations within the docks.

Left: On 17th September 1958 class E1 0-6-0T No.32689 is shunting in the New Docks. On the cab roof is the radio-telephone equipment for the handset inside the cab. No.32689 spent two spells at the docks, first between 1943 and 1950 before returning in 1955, remaining until it was withdrawn in February 1960.
(Photo: H.W. Robinson Copyright J.F. Hyde Steam Archive)

Right: *USA* class No.30065 in the Old Docks also on 17th September 1958 with at least one member of the crew posing for the camera.
(Photo: H.W. Robinson Copyright J.F. Hyde Steam Archive)

Left: Co-ordination between loco crew and the shunter as class E1 0-6-0 tank No.32689 shunts in the Old Docks on 26th June 1957.
(Photo: R.C. Riley Copyright Transport Treasury)

Below: The crews of two *USA* tanks enjoy a break between shunting on 8th July 1950. No.30072 is in early British Railways livery, while the locomotive on the left is unidentified. Happily No.30072 was preserved when it was withdrawn in 1967 and is now on the Keighley and Worth Valley Railway.
(Photo: Copyright R.K. Blencowe Collection)

Left: An overseas traveller, class E4 0-6-2 tank locomotive No.32510, which spent some time on the Isle of Wight in the late 1940s, is seen in the New Docks on 9th September 1961, a year before it was withdrawn. Beside it is class E2 No.32105 withdrawn the same month as No.32510 just after the arrival of the new diesel shunters.
(Photo: A.R. Grierson Copyright Stephenson Locomotive Society Collection)

The Harbour Board Lines

Above: *USA* tank No.30068 passes across the entrance to the Royal Pier on the link line to the New Docks with a handsignalman on duty. No.30068 was withdrawn in March 1963. (Photo: Copyright Colour-Rail 342245)

As mentioned previously the Harbour Commissioners were established in 1803 to take control of the port and Southampton Water, as well as taking charge of the early port's quays. They were responsible for rebuilding the Town and Watergate Quays, and also the building of what was to become known as the Royal Pier. Now ships could access the port at any state of the tide, and so routes to the Isle of Wight, Channel Islands and France could be developed.

At this point the plans for the London and Southampton Railway (L&SR) were being developed, to which the Harbour Commissioners initially objected on the grounds that the proposed terminus was too far from the quay. At the same time it was realised that Southampton needed to develop a full scale docks facility if it was to reach its potential as a port. However, the Harbour Commissioners were limited by their Act of Parliament in how much money they could raise for new facilities.

Therefore, they had to stand by and watch a new docks company being formed, and the new facilities developed, which in many ways were taking the place of theirs. This led to an uneasy relationship between the two companies, which at certain points was outrightly hostile, such as over the Harbour Commissioners' proposed tramway.

The Tramway

On 25th May 1845, a few years after the opening of both the L&SR and the Outer Dock, the Harbour commissioners considered the building of a tramway from the quay to the LSWR station so that goods could be transferred between the two. In March 1847, they approached the SDC about the possibility of the line passing through the docks estate to link with the SDC's connection with the LSWR, as the railway company would not permit the construction of a second line into their station. This the SDC refused. As a result the Commissioners got permission to build the line along Canute Road and connect it to the line to the station by means of a turntable.

To say that the SDC was not happy with this arrangement is something of an understatement. There was a whole stream of complaints, particularly when construction of the tramway got underway in June 1847. They were concerned that the tramway was being built on their land, although actually it was 10ft from their boundary. In addition, they argued that the ground levels were wrong for the turntable, but all to no avail as operations began on 31st December 1847. However, even then they were taking legal advice in March 1848 as to whether the tramway could be regarded as a 'nuisance'.

The tramway was worked by the Harbour Commissioners with horses, but in 1851 the line was leased to the LSWR for £20 per annum with the Commissioners remaining responsible for maintenance. It was still horse-worked. In 1853 the Town Quay was extended by 300ft, along with the sidings on it.

Major changes came in the 1870s, when a new line was built from Canute Road into the Docks station doing away with the turntable. The tramway was also extended onto the Royal Pier. Here a simple station with a run-round loop was constructed, which opened on 25th September 1871, at a total cost of £3,000.

Now a passenger service from the Docks station to the Isle of Wight ferries was introduced with three carriages, one 1st class, one 2nd class and a guards van provided. Although only a few hundred yards in length, the extension, and the provision of this new service to link to the Isle of Wight, was seen as so significant that the LSWR chairman highlighted it in his report to shareholders on more than one occasion.

By now the tramway had new owners, as the Southampton Harbour and Pier Board succeeded the Commissioners in 1863. From then on the tramway was increasingly known as the 'Harbour Board Lines'.

Steam Power

Freight traffic was booming with over 500 wagon journeys in November 1872, rising to more than 1,000 in November 1875, still all horse-worked. By this time the docks were primarily handling goods from foreign shores, and so the coastal traffic was being worked via the Town Quay and the tramway. With this level of traffic it is not surprising

that in 1876 the LSWR applied for permission from Southampton Council to operate steam locomotives on the line.

After a trial with one of the docks locomotives, the Council consented to an initial period of one year. This was with the provisions that the speed of the trains was limited to 5mph. A flagman with a bell was also to be provided as a warning whenever the train crossed a public right of way. Any locomotive should be equipped with powerful brakes and exhaust steam was to be discharged into its tanks. Finally that any engine should not exceed 13 tons in weight.

As a result the LSWR ordered an 0-4-0T from Shanks & Son of Arbroath at a cost of £995, which entered service on 21st September 1876 named *Southampton*. It was followed by a second also supplied by Shanks in 1877 named *Cowes*. These engines had a curious appearance as they were fitted with condensing pipes. This was to fulfil the requirement that exhaust steam should be discharged into the tanks. They were joined in 1879 by a third locomotive, bought secondhand to a slightly different design, named *Ritzebuttel*.

While the Council had laid down a maximum speed of 5mph for engines on the lines, what nobody appreciated was that this did not supersede the provisions of the Locomotive Act of 1865. This Act laid down a maximum speed of 4mph for locomotives proceeding along a public highway, and 2mph when travelling through towns and villages. The LSWR found this out the hard way when they lost a case of speeding on the line in 1881.

To counteract this The Southampton Harbour Act of 1882 contained a number of clauses relating to the running of

The Town Quay Lines circa 1866

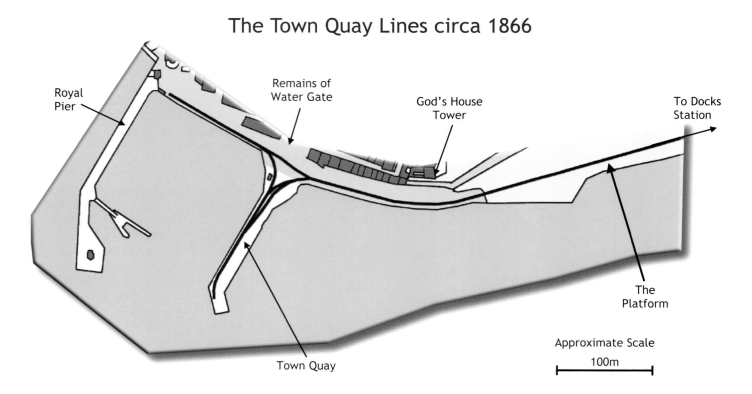

Above: A fine view of *Ritzebuttel* at Eastleigh showing its condensing pipes. These transferred much of the steam exhaust back into the saddle tank to conform with the regulations originally imposed for steam engines on the Harbour Board lines.

(Photo: Real Photographs Copyright NRM/SSPL)

trains, and the design of the locomotives involved. These included provisions that fires on the locomotives needed to be hidden, and that the locomotives were to be fitted with 'life-guards' to push aside obstructions. Examination of the photographs of the locomotives in use on the Harbour Board lines fails to show any particular design of the latter devices being fitted, which perhaps leads to the thought that this clause was ignored.

In 1884 the LSWR applied for permission to ease the curve on the exit from the Docks station in order to permit the running of six-wheel carriages on the line. This possibly indicates when through workings started, but a timetabled passenger service did not appear in the LSWR public timetable until 1891.

Further changes came in the early 1890s when the Royal Pier was rebuilt in cast iron, 1,000ft in length, and covered railway platforms constructed, with the new pier opening on 2nd June 1892. The Town Quay was also extended by 850ft and rebuilt in reinforced concrete, with two-storey warehouses constructed along the centreline. In addition, electric cranes were installed, the first in Great Britain.

Further Developments

When in 1892 the LSWR took over the docks, some of the previous tensions between the two enterprises were

eased, although the Town Quay and Royal Pier lines still remained the property of the Harbour Board. As a result of the new relationship in 1893 a new connection was laid into the docks from the Harbour Board lines, so that trains could run from the Docks station through the docks and onto the line to Town Quay at *The Platform* without having to pass along Canute Road, which was what the Harbour Commissioners had requested in 1847! This allowed bogie coaches to operate on the line to Royal Pier.

A few years later another loop line was laid at *The Platform* to increase line capacity. Around the turn of the century the line was extended beyond the Royal Pier for the transportation of material excavated from the White Star Dock and Trafalgar Dry Dock to be used in reclamation projects.

By 1902 *Cowes* and *Ritzebuttel* were superseded by *Clausentum* from the docks fleet with *Southampton* being the standby engine. From 1911 class C14 2-2-0T's began to be used, which were ideally suited to the tight curves on the Quay because of their short wheelbase, and were to remain a feature of the line until 1959.

Passenger Services

At this time there were through carriages operating between Waterloo and the Royal Pier specifically to make

Left: The rebuilt Pier station was still a relatively simple affair with two wooden platforms and basic shelters. It merely serving as a transit point for the Isle of Wight ferries, rather than being a destination in itself. The advertising changed through the years, with a number of firms having their names emblazoned across various parts of the structure.

(Commercial Postcard)

The Harbour Board Lines circa 1908

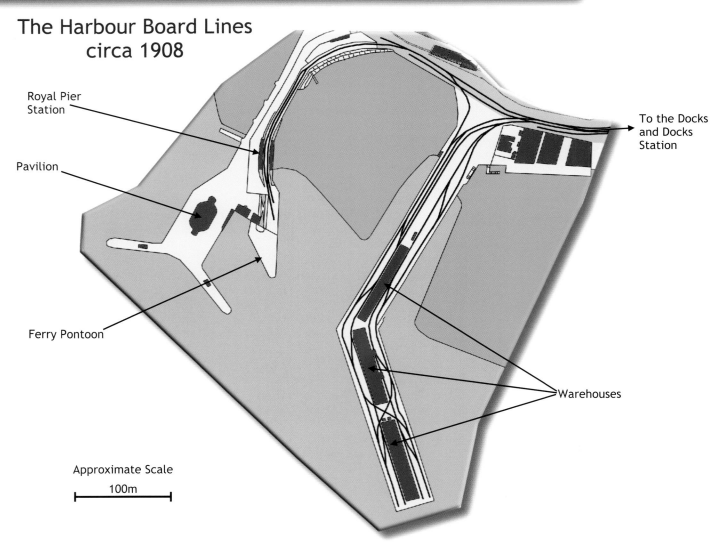

Royal Pier Station

Pavilion

Ferry Pontoon

To the Docks and Docks Station

Warehouses

Approximate Scale

100m

connections with the Isle of Wight steamers. In the summer of 1909 trains from Waterloo on weekdays at 5.35 am, 7.40 am, 11.40 am, 12.50 pm, 3.00 pm and 6.00 pm ran through to Royal Pier, with return workings at 8.15 am, 10.50 am, 12.55 pm, 2.45 pm, 4.50 pm and 7.10 pm. All of these services also called at the Docks station. In addition there was a through working at 2.35 pm with coaches being attached to a Waterloo train at Southampton West having been brought up from Royal Pier without stopping at the Docks station.

However, from December 1909 H12 and H13 steam railmotors took over passenger services, and the through coaches ceased, the railmotors shuttling between the Pier and Docks stations. In the summer of 1914 weekday services were run to connect with the 5.35 am, 7.40 am, 11.40 am, 12.50 pm, 2.55 pm, and 6.00 pm trains from Waterloo. In the reverse direction trains left Royal Pier at 8.15 am, 10.52 am, 12.55 pm, 2.35 pm, 4.50 pm, and 7.10 pm. But this would be the last of these services, because with the outbreak of war the service was suspended never to be reinstated.

One locomotive to see service on the Town Quay line at this time will be known to readers of *Southern Rails on the Isle of Wight*, as one of the two ex-London, Brighton and South Coast Railway *Terrier* locomotives the LSWR owned, No.734, worked on the Harbour Board lines in 1912 and 1913. It was then sold to the Freshwater, Yarmouth and Newport Railway, becoming their No.2,

and later absorbed into SR stock as W2 *Freshwater*. It is now at work on the Isle of Wight Steam Railway.

During the First World War the line was used for troop movements to and from both the Pier and Quay. Late in the war there was also a connection to the train ferry terminal. But after the war, around 1921, a ship collided with the Royal Pier, severely damaging the railway, and it was closed. By this time too the services to and from Town Quay were being routed through the docks estate. Eventually the length of the tramway along Canute Road was abandoned. The section of the old tramway which ran beside Platform Road, where two loops and a siding had been laid before the war, now became effectively a set of sidings. This became a picturesque location for photography with the background of trees and Queen's Park.

The Southern

At the Grouping the Southern took over operation of the line from the LSWR, but it still remained the property of the Harbour Board. Now it was solely a goods operation to the Town Quay operated primarily by the C14 tanks, Nos. 0741 and 0744, which were rebuilt as 0-4-0T's, being allocated to the task. By the mid 1920s around 170 wagon journeys took place along the line each day.

Town Quay was a significant contributor to the economic life of the port at that time. Ships regularly sailed from

Above: Many commercial postcards were produced showing the pier and station from the landward side. This one has been chosen because it shows two trains in the station which would have occurred around 2.30 pm in the early years of the twentieth century. The train on the left is headed by *Southampton* and the one of the right by *Clausentum* (distinguishable by the cutouts to the cab), one train was a through working to Waterloo via the Docks station, while the other ran to Waterloo via Southampton West. On the right the original toll-house is seen, the posters advertising promenade concerts and *The Fantastics* for the delectation of those attending the pier pavilion.
(Commercial Postcard)

Above: A pre-Grouping view of the Town Quay with an impressive array of wagons on it. One of the docks 0-4-0 tanks can just be made out shunting the sidings. In the foreground can be seen the temporary line that was used to shift spoil from the excavation of the Trafalgar Dry Dock for use in land reclamation further up Western Esplanade. This dates this photo to the early 1900s. (Commercial Postcard)

Left: The *Silver Spray* was a 42 ton spritsail barge built in Rochester in 1898, which had a number of owners through to the 1930s. It is seen here next to the quay wall between the Town Quay and the Royal Pier, with the original Royal Pier toll house in the distance. A number of LSWR wagons can be seen on the siding, making this likely to be a pre-Grouping scene. (Photo: Bert Moody Collection)

Below: *Clausentum* and a train at the Pier station in the early years of the twentieth century. The first coach of the train is a passenger luggage van stood with its doors open.
(Photo: Lens of Sutton Collection)

Left: The Harbour Board building to the left of the picture had probably only recently been completed in this photograph, taken c1930, showing the approaches to Town Quay. In the background is the impressive Floating Dry Dock with the Cunard liner *Berengaria* undergoing repairs.

(Commercial Postcard)

Right: A mid 1930s view of Town Quay. The work on the new quay wall between the Quay and the Royal Pier has been completed, and also the rebuilding of the nearest Quay warehouses carried out.

(Photo: Southern Railway courtesy BRB)

Left: Looking just to the right of the view above shows the extent of the sidings along what is now Town Quay Road. Where the furthest siding was is now the Red Funnel terminal for the Isle of Wight.

(Commercial Postcard)

there to Aberdeen, Belfast, Bristol, Cardiff, Cork, Dublin, Falmouth, Glasgow, Greenock, Hull, King's Lynn, Liverpool, London, Middlesbrough, Newcastle-Upon-Tyne, Plymouth, Swansea, and Waterford. In addition there were services to Norway, Sweden, Belgium, Germany and France, as well as the regular services to and from the Isle of Wight.

In 1930 the annual amount of cargo handled on the Town Quay amounted to some 200,000 tons, among which were cargos of timber, agricultural fertilizers, flour, ice, oil cake, cement, steel plates and materials for shipbuilding, mineral waters, whisky, oats and potatoes. Significant amounts of cargo were trans-shipped both to and from the docks as well as being distributed via the SR throughout the hinterland. Passengers also made use of coastal and other sailings, in order to connect with the liners sailing from the docks.

It was at this time that the Harbour Board lines took on a new significance, as they became the main access to the construction site for the New Docks extension. As mentioned previously this commenced in 1927 with the construction of a new quay wall between the Town Quay and the Pier, and between the Pier and the former train ferry jetty. This was extended north-west to permit the reclamation of what would become the main contractor's base for the building of the New Docks.

As already mentioned the old pier toll-house had to be demolished to permit the laying of a new rail connection to the New Docks. In addition, the increased use of the Harbour Board's lines for the new traffic, led to some capacity problems which caused conflicts with the services to Town Quay. It also led to new agreement between the SR and the Harbour Board being signed in 1931. Under this not only did the SR have to pay for the maintenance of the line, they had to pay the Harbour Board £500 per year for its use until five years after the docks extension was opened. They were, though, permitted to keep the tolls.

Once the new berths were open the Harbour Board lines and the new connection continued to be the only rail access until the junction at Millbrook was completed in 1935. Therefore, there continued to be significant traffic along the route for many years. In 1938 the agreement with the Harbour Board was renewed for three years, but this time the payment was £750 annually emphasising the number of trains that passed over the route.

During the Second World War some coastal shipping continued to use the Town Quay, and so it remained open. It also played its role in receiving refugees from the invasion of France and Belgium, and of course in the run-up and follow-on to D-Day. As will be seen, two rail embarkation points were established close to the Royal

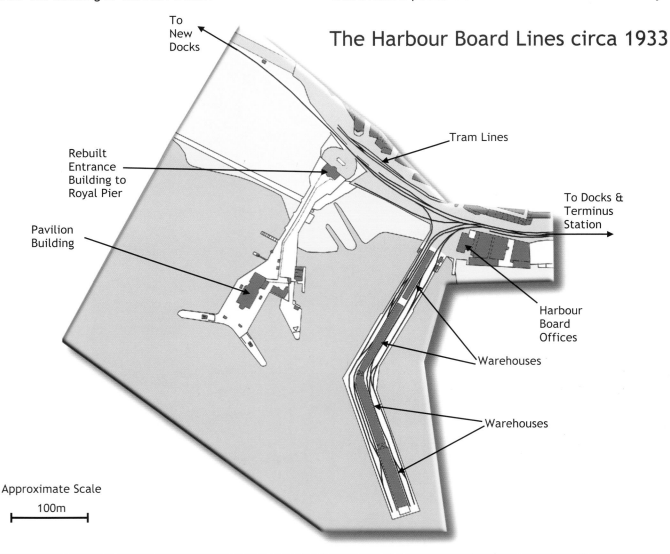

To New Docks

The Harbour Board Lines circa 1933

Tram Lines

Rebuilt Entrance Building to Royal Pier

To Docks & Terminus Station

Pavilion Building

Harbour Board Offices

Warehouses

Warehouses

Approximate Scale

100m

Right and Below: Two aerial photographs probably taken in the early 1920s of the area around the Royal Pier and Town Quay showing some of the Harbour Board lines. The steam crane on the approach lines to the Quay is particularly worth noting. Also note the absence of the Harbour Board offices building by Town Quay in the lower picture.
(Commercial Postcards)

Town Quay

Original Royal Pier Toll House

South Western Hotel

Harland and Wolff works

Town Quay

Town Quay

Royal Pier

Right: Giving the lie to the myth that every locomotive was always immaculately turned out pre-nationalisation, class C14 No.0744, now rebuilt as an 0-4-0T, shunts at Town Quay sometime between July 1925 when it was painted in Southern livery and August 1931 when it was repainted and also renumbered as No.3744.
(Photo: Bert Moody Collection)

Pier as part of this operation. There was also an occasion in July 1941 when the main line through Southampton was blocked. Trains were diverted through the New and Old Docks, making use of the link and Harbour Board lines in the process.

Post-War Operations

After the war of course the docks and its railways were nationalised. However, the Harbour Board remained, and, although their lines were now operated by British Railways, in reality relatively little changed. Still the C14s were in charge although occasionally a *USA* tank could be seen at work on the line, and there was significant traffic passing along the link line from the New Docks.

However, by the late 1950s the C14s were showing their age, and in 1957 both Nos.0741 and 0744 now BR Nos. 30588 and 30589 were withdrawn. In their place came another C14 which had been serving at Redbridge Permanent Way Works as No.77s. It was to serve until

1959, when it was replaced by Class 04 0-6-0 diesel mechanical shunter No.11224, later D2218, which was adapted for the tight curves on the quay lines. Other members of the class were also employed over the lines.

Slowly through the 1960s the traffic declined until the freight service to the Town Quay was withdrawn on 4th May 1970. However, the link line between the two docks continued to function until October 1979, when it too succumbed. In the meantime the Harbour Board finally became part of British Transport Docks Board on 1st August 1969.

Today almost all trace of the old Harbour Board lines has gone. The Royal Pier is derelict and in danger of collapse, save for the 1930s entrance, now a restaurant. Meanwhile the Town Quay has been redeveloped with apartments and shops, although Red Funnel catamaran sailings to Cowes and the Hythe Ferry still operate from there. There is though now talk of a major redevelopment for the area which could transform things yet again.

Above: A major change to the Harbour Board lines came in the 1960s when diesel power was introduced. Here class 04 D2290 is seen at work near Town Quay on 9th September 1965. (Photo: H.W. Robinson Copyright J.F. Hyde Steam Archive)

Left: E1 class No.32151 with a goods train on the link line from the New Docks in the late afternoon on 3rd September 1959. Those Sotonians of my generation or older will be familiar with the Southampton Corporation Guy Arab bus stood at the bus stop. No.32151 would only survive in service until January 1960.
(Photo: R. Amos Copyright Kidderminster Railway Museum)

Right: Class C14 No.30588 shunts at Town Quay on 23rd December 1950. The photo on page 116 shows this scene today.

(Photo: K.G. Carr Copyright P. Fidczuk)

Left: Not the best photo certainly but it shows the scene at Town Quay not long after the war, when some of the bomb damage is evident on the left. No.30588 is shunting on the right while class E1 No.32156 is in charge of a rake of empty coaching stock running through to the New Docks on 23rd December 1950.
(Photo: K.G. Carr Copyright P. Fidczuk)

Left: Q class No.30542 heads towards the Old Docks having travelled along the link line from the New Docks with a pipe train on 5th October 1957.

(Photo: Colin Hogg Courtesy Bluebell Railway Museum Archive)

Above: The chalk graffiti on the front of Q1 class No.33021 confirms the date of this photo as being taken in August 1958, as it hauls a train loaded with timber from the New Docks about to enter the Old Docks at Gate No.1. *Six-Five Special* ran on the BBC between 1957 and 1958, but who PAUL was has sadly been lost in the midst of time.

(Photographer Unknown)

Left: Looking along the route of the line to Town Quay in March 2012.

Left: Rolling stock on Town Quay Road in the 1930s. Tram tracks are on the right, what the object is loaded on the well wagon is something of a mystery.
(Photo: Southampton Record Office/Associated British Ports)

Right: In the early years of the twentieth century *Ritzebuttel* heads a train of bogie stock from the pier to the Docks station past the remains of the God's House Tower.
(Photo: H. Brain Courtesy J. Brown)

Left: Again in the early years of the twentieth century and again probably *Ritzebuttel* heads a train up the old line along Canute Road before entering the Docks station.
(Photo: Bert Moody Collection)

Left: The loco and shunting crew pose with class C14 No.30588 at the sidings by Dock Gate No.1 on 26th June 1957.
(Photo: R.C. Riley Copyright Transport Treasury)

Above: *USA* class No.30071 shunting near Dock Gate No.1 with class C14 No.30588 on the right on Christmas Eve 1952.
(Photo: K.G. Carr Copyright P. Fidczuk)

Left: The same scene in March 2012.

Above: In November 1967 D2989, later No.07005, passes over the approach road to the Royal Pier with a transfer freight to the Western Docks.
(Photo: John H. Bird Copyright Southern-Images)

Below: A Class 07 at Town Quay on 9th April 1973.
(Photo: K.G. Carr Copyright P. Fidczuk)

Left: Construction of the classically designed Harbour Board offices building began in 1924, and it is now a casino.

Right: The rebuilt Royal Pier entrance building is now a restaurant, but sadly the rest of the pier is crumbling into decay.

Left: Some of the surviving buildings opposite Town Quay, including the remains of the original Water Gate in March 2012.

Right: Town Quay from the seaward side on 23rd August 2012.

Train Ferries and Ambulance Trains

Above: A view showing a US Army Ambulance train on the train ferry jetty on 11th April 1918. The locomotive is Kerr Stuart 0-6-0T No.11 while the sixteen carriages were originally constructed by the Lancashire and Yorkshire Railway. Between the third and fourth coaches the pinnacle of the Royal Pier toll house can just be seen. (Photo: Copyright NRM/SSPL)

The First World War

Supply lines are always a concern in any military campaign. So it was for the British in the First World War, particularly as the fighting was being carried out across the Channel. At the same time railways were still the main form of land transportation. As a result early in 1917 it was decided to instigate a train ferry service between Britain and France. The advantages of this were that vital supplies could be directly loaded in wagons on to the ferries and rapidly offloaded for onward travel to their destination. In addition, extra locomotives, carriages and wagons could be supplied to the French and other railway networks. One particular concern was to enable the transportation of Ambulance trains to the Continent for use in evacuating the wounded.

Two British ports were chosen as the starting points for these services, Richborough in Kent and Southampton. In the case of Southampton the plan was for a service to operate to Dieppe. Three ferries were ordered, imaginatively named *TF1*, *TF2* and *TF3*. Train ferry *TF2* was assigned to Southampton. They were all designed to take a total of 54 10 ton wagons on four parallel tracks.

At Southampton work on the new facilities for the service began in August 1917. Just to the north-west of the Royal Pier a 100 yard long masonry jetty was constructed from which a 100 yard long timber viaduct was built. At the end of this was a link-span to enable loading to take place whatever the state of the tide. However, it seems as if some of the early sailings took place before the link-span

was completed, which would have meant that loading would have had to have taken place during a short tidal 'window' when the deck of the ferry could be lined up with the jetty.

To link the jetty with the main rail network the nearby Harbour Board lines were initially ignored, probably due to the demands already being made on them by the wartime traffic. Instead a connecting line, double track for most of its length, was laid from Southampton West station along the then shore line past the power station, lido and Pirelli cable works. This meant that a significant amount of land reclamation had to be undertaken. As it passed the lido and the Pirelli works a loop line was added to each of the running lines. In addition, sidings were laid into the Pirelli works.

Just beyond the Pirelli works a thirteen-road marshalling yard capable of handling 500 wagons was constructed. From this a further eight sidings, that could take 200 wagons, were laid parallel to Western Esplanade. In addition, there was a single road leading to an engine shed built to accommodate the two locomotives assigned to the yard and jetty. Meanwhile back at West station another set of seven sidings was constructed between Western Esplanade and the power station. All-in-all this was a very extensive system (see plan on page 119).

As already stated two locomotives were assigned to the ferry yards. The first was an 0-6-0 tank locomotive, which was a Kerr Stuart *Victory* class locomotive built in May 1917, and numbered No.11. The second was an unidentified Peckett 0-4-0 saddle tank.

The first sailings to Dieppe took place in December 1917, but the work on the yards and link-span were not completed until March 1918. However, the service proved a success, and it was proposed to start a second service to Cherbourg. In order for this to happen a fourth ferry was obtained for the fleet, named *TF4*. In this case the ferry was brought secondhand from Canada, although it was originally built by Cammell-Laird at Birkenhead in 1914 and named the *Leonard*.

It was 307ft long and 65ft wide with a 30ft high girder superstructure, which allowed the deck to move up or down by 18ft. This meant it did not need a link-span, but the three lines of track on the deck prompted a new loading berth to be constructed on the south-east side of the jetty. At the same time a line was laid to Town Quay in connection with a barge service to France. *TF4* was capable of carrying 39 10 ton wagons, and entered service on 6th November 1918, less than a week before the Armistice came into force.

However, ferry services continued until March 1919 when all services ceased, *TF4* having only made twelve return crossings since entering service. How effective the service was is a matter of some controversy. Certainly the figures are impressive totalling eight locomotives, 42 coaches and 6,763 wagons exported, and 272 locomotives and 1,250 wagons shipped back during the life of the service. However, it was stated that the service was at times restricted due to a lack of escort vessels for the Channel crossing.

After the war *TF4* was sold and converted to an oil tanker called the *Limax*. *TF1*, *TF2* and *TF3* were sold and eventually were used on the route from Harwich to Zebrugge, but *TF2* was destined to return to Southampton during World War Two (see later). Meanwhile the infrastructure was dismantled except for the jetty, which remained until the 1920s when it was used as a base for the New Docks extension. It was finally demolished at a cost of £24,000 in 1935. The connection at Southampton West also remained until the New Docks were built being used for the transportation of material to the site until the link line from Town Quay was completed.

First World War Ambulance Trains

The development of Ambulance trains in effect started with the provision in 1900 of the 'Netley Coaches' for injured troops returning from the Boer War to Southampton for transport to the Military Hospital at Netley. This was taken further by the War Railway Council, who in conjunction with the London and North Western Railway drew up plans for the conversion of existing coaches for service as Ambulance trains.

This enabled twelve army ambulance trains, supplied by various railway companies, to be made available at the beginning of the war, one of which was supplied by the LSWR. On arrival at Southampton some modifications were ordered to the trains, which were carried out at Eastleigh between trips. Each of the trains retained their originating companies liveries, with red crosses on the sides and roofs, and set numbers in large numerals on the sides of the end carriages. The first trip by one of these trains in service was made on 28th August 1914.

During 1914 Southampton was the sole port used for these returning casualties, but later use was made of the facilities at Dover, with six trains being transferred there.

Left: One of the original train ferries, presumably *TF2*, with a US Army Ambulance train No.60 being loaded on board via the link-span to the jetty in the background. The capstans used to tie the vehicles down during the voyage can be seen between the tracks.
(Photo: Copyright NRM/SSPL)

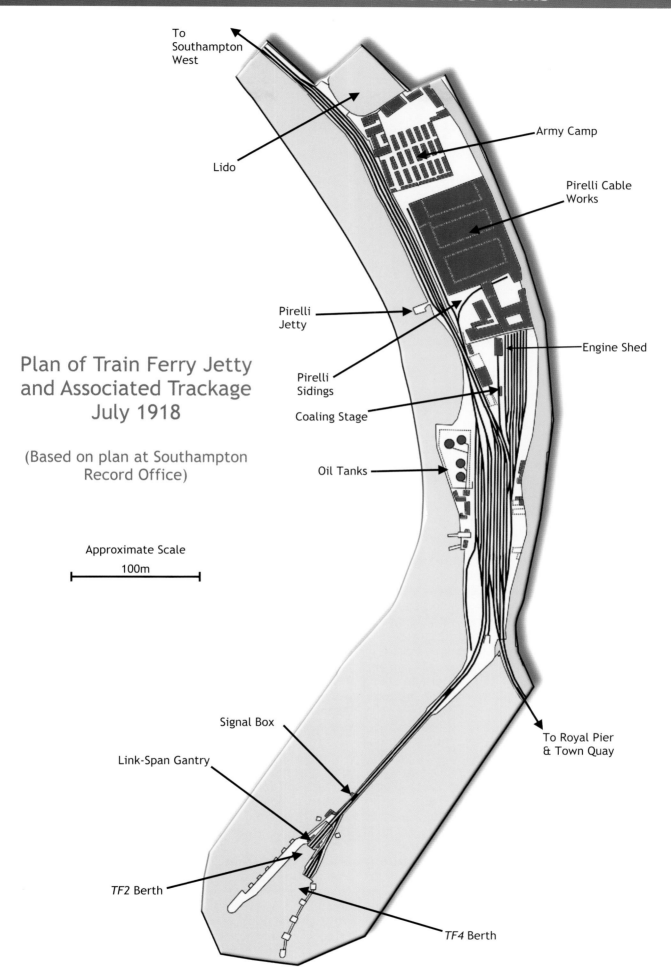

To Southampton West

Army Camp

Pirelli Cable Works

Lido

Pirelli Jetty

Engine Shed

Plan of Train Ferry Jetty and Associated Trackage July 1918

(Based on plan at Southampton Record Office)

Pirelli Sidings

Coaling Stage

Oil Tanks

Approximate Scale

100m

To Royal Pier & Town Quay

Signal Box

Link-Span Gantry

TF2 Berth

TF4 Berth

Above: A view taken shortly after the end of the First World War showing the train ferry jetty at Southampton. In the original berth is probably *HMS Hermione* being stored before disposal, while at its special berth is *TF4*. The signal box which controlled the jetty can be seen about three-quarters of the way along its length, and also one of the signals can be made out. Royal Pier station can also be seen in the centre-right of the photo with two paddle steamers moored alongside the Pier. Looking across the background the River Itchen can be seen and on the right the Inner and Outer Docks as well as Town Quay. (Commercial Postcard)

Additional trains were also provided for service in Europe.

One of the features of the docks facilities at Southampton was the ability to provide heating. Therefore, the transit and cargo sheds used for the transhipment of casualties from the ships to the trains were heated. Then the trains, which themselves had been heated by the docks system, were shunted into the sheds for loading. A simple system was used of loading the trains which had the furthest to travel first, casualties having been pre-assigned trains to facilities as far as possible in their home area. The aim was to disembark all patients on the day of the ship's arrival and the trains took them all over Britain including Scotland.

Of course the numbers of casualties, like so many connected with the First World War are staggering. Between 24th August 1914 and 31st December 1918 there were 7,822 Ambulance train journeys from Southampton with over 1,250,000 patients on board. Key battles brought increased numbers of casualties, the *Aquitania* returned with 5,000 casualties from the Gallipoli campaign in 1915, which required twenty trains to transfer them to their receiving hospitals. The battle of the Somme led to 151 trains departing from Southampton during the week leading up to 9th July 1916, 29 on one day, carrying a total of over 30,000 patients.

More trains were added to the fleet particularly for service in Europe as the war progressed. Later after the USA entered the war nineteen trains of sixteen coaches each were built by a number of companies for the US Army. As will have been seen in the preceding pictures at least one of these was transported to Dieppe on the Southampton train ferry.

The Second World War

During the Second World War train ferries were again to be seen at Southampton, initially in the form of *TF's 1, 2 & 3*, which were pressed once more into service as part of Operation Dynamo to evacuate troops from Dunkirk. *TF2* was in fact sunk by German gunfire on 10th June 1940 when evacuating troops from the mouth of the River Somme. *TF1* and *TF3* were rebuilt for further war service becoming HMS *Iris* and HMS *Daffodil* respectively.

Iris survived the war, being rebuilt once more in 1946, and renamed as *Essex Ferry* serving once more on the Harwich to Zebrugge route until 1957. *Daffodil* was not so fortunate, being sunk when it hit a mine while carrying locomotives from Southampton to Cherbourg in March 1945.

This last event pointed up the role that the Southampton train ferries had in the operations surrounding D-Day in 1944. There were at least three loading places set up around the port for varying sizes of ship. To the north-west of the King George V dry dock berth 109 was established for the largest of the train ferries to operate from the port. These included three SR ships *Hampton Ferry*, *Shepperton Ferry* and *Twickenham Ferry* which

Above: One of the London and North Western Railway personnel coaches No.5006 that was part of Home Ambulance Train No.8. This set entered service in October 1914 and is seen at Southampton Docks later in the war as the original white roof has been repainted. The carriage to the left is probably No.2111A, which was added to the set in 1916, and was originally a sleeping car that had been converted to a diner in 1903. In Army service it contained a kitchen and pantry with seating for seventeen.

Right: A fine portrait shot of one of the LSWR wagons used for internal movements in the docks. It is seen at the north-west corner of the Inner Dock, while in the background is requisitioned hospital ship E0682. Sadly the author has not been able to ascertain the civilian name for this ship. On the left quayside part of the lifting conveyor on the grain elevator can also be made out.

Left: The three photographs on this page were taken by a Lieutenant Infield who judging by the spelling of his rank was an American (Women nurses in the American Army did not have officer rank at this time). In the set of photographs he took there is a concentration on the nursing staff that had presumably disembarked from the hospital ships. Here is one pair of nurses in a hired cab waiting to depart from the docks. Judging from the name on the suitcase one of the occupants is a G.E. Davies, perhaps the one offering a flirtatious smile! The humour probably belies the relief of being back in England, and the dedication of all the medical staff, who treated casualties at every stage back from the front line, must never be forgotten.

(Photos on this page: Lt Infield)

had been built in 1934-35 for the Dover to Dunkirk service. They were fitted with rear gantries by which they could load or unload rolling stock and even turn locomotives.

At the north-west corner of Mayflower Park by berth 101 a loading area for converted tank landing craft was established, while between the Royal Pier and Town Quay tracks were laid for wagons to be loaded into other landing craft type vessels. After the war there was talk of establishing a train ferry service between Southampton and Cherbourg. This, though, came to nothing, the landing stages were quickly removed, and nearly all traces of their existence obliterated.

Second World War Ambulance Trains

Upon the outbreak of the Second World War again Ambulance trains were constructed this time using LMS coaches as a basis. Two trains of nine coaches were converted for home use. In addition, four sets of sixteen carriages each were exported to Europe either through Southampton or Harwich. This was followed in 1940 by

twelve further sets of carriages for use in Britain, and thirteen which were sent to France. All of the trains that were sent to France from both batches were lost in the retreat across Europe to Dunkirk.

Later in the war a further 35 train sets were requisitioned for service in various overseas theatres of war. Finally when the United States entered the war extra train sets were provided for the US Army from 1943, ten fourteen-coach sets being made available, and one fifteen-coach rake. Six of these train sets were ferried to France via Southampton following D-Day with the rest crossing the channel by alternative routes.

Other stock was converted for use as Casualty Evacuation Trains to transport patients from major cities to free up hospital beds for air raid victims. Elsewhere nine ex-LSWR dining saloons were converted for use as self-contained ambulance coaches. In the late 1950s two of these coaches were used to transport patients to Lourdes, while others found their way to various military railways. Two of these carriages have been preserved and were last known to be at the Pontypool and Blaenavon Railway.

Left: US Army Transportation Corps locomotive No.2347 being loaded onto *Hampton Ferry* at Southampton on 12th August 1944 along with with a train of tank wagons. This photograph was taken at the specially created berth 109 to the north-west of the King George V Graving Dock.
(Photo: Bert Moody Collection Courtesy BRB)

Right: The lifting gantry in use to turn 2-8-0 *Consolidation* class locomotive No.2255 prior to loading onto *Hampton Ferry* on 18th August 1944. No.2255 along with No.2347 above were members of the S160 class of locomotives built by Baldwin, Alco and Lima for the US Army Transporation Corps. Over 2,000 examples were built and saw service in Europe, Africa, Asia and South America, as well as in Great Britain. Several have been preserved and one, No.6046, which saw service in France and Hungary, has recently been overhauled at the Churnet Valley Railway in Staffordshire, where its sister locomotive No.5197 is also based.
(Photo: Bert Moody Collection Courtesy BRB)

Left: The view from *Twickenham Ferry* at berth 109 on 13th August 1944 showing the entrance to the King George V Dry Dock on the left and berth 108 in the background. The array of different craft moored at the quays is worth noting, as well as the barrage balloons moored overhead.
(Photo: Bert Moody Collection Courtesy BRB)

Right: The background to this photo was obliterated by the censor, but the most likely location is the loading area created at the north-west corner of Mayflower Park by berth 101. The locomotive is WD179 ex-GWR No.2466. This was originally a class 2300 0-6-0 Dean goods locomotive, which was one of a hundred requisitioned at the outbreak of World War Two. No.2466 was one of ten fitted with pannier tanks and condensing apparatus, which can be seen in the photograph, although still retaining their tenders. Clearly the loco crew are feeling relaxed about the task in hand.
(Photo: Bert Moody Collection)

Left: These POW's were probably not in the mood to attend one of the Royal Pier dances as they were unloaded at Southampton. Just to the middle left of the photo one of the temporary tracks that were laid down to the water's edge for loading boats can be seen.
(Photo: Bert Moody Collection)

Northam Wharves

Above: A view probably taken to mark the passing of the old and the beginning of the new. Le Dansk had just taken over the operation of the Northam Wharves line in 1934 after the Dixon & Cardus mill closed. They immediately purchased a new internal combustion four-wheel drive locomotive from Muir Hill Engineering Ltd to replace the John Fowler 0-4-2T *Nicholson* seen on the right which was scrapped shortly after this photo was taken.

(Photo: Photographer Unknown J.R. Fairman Collection Kidderminster Railway Museum)

According to a newspaper report in 1840 the LSWR built some coke ovens at Northam, just south of Mount Pleasant crossing, where it apparently owned the freehold to some of the waterfront land, with the intent of claiming a stake in the coal merchant business. To service the ovens a tramway was laid to Northam Quay just east of Northam Bridge, and also probably connected to the main line. By 1845 there was also a siding serving a 'Bone and Linseed Crushing Mill', which made artificial fertilizer and was owned by Messrs. Twynam.

One of the partners in the business was Edward Dixon, who had served under Joseph Locke as Resident Engineer on the construction of the L&SR, and who was involved in the construction of a number of early railways. By 1852 he had returned to Southampton and formed a partnership with Thomas Cardus to take over Twynam's works under the title of Dixon & Cardus.

By 1866 the system had been changed with the connection to the coke ovens removed. However, now the system had been extended eastward to serve Northam Sawmills, owned by Driver & Co., and Northam Iron Works and shipyard occupied by Day, Summers and Co. previously based at Millbrook Foundry. A new addition was the Le Dansk margarine factory established in 1891. Before the end of the century there was also a connection into the Bridge Foundry, west of Northam Bridge.

Up until this point horses worked the line, but early in the

twentieth century, not long after their Redbridge factory had also moved to Northam, Dixon & Cardus obtained a 0-4-0 saddle tank built by Manning Wardle. This locomotive had originally been built in 1866, and completely rebuilt in 1879. After the rebuild the locomotive was owned by Lucas & Aird in Bristol, before being purchased by Dixon & Cardus in 1911 and named *Eva*. It served at Northam for eight years including the First World War, being replaced in 1919, and sold the following year to the Petters Westland Works at Yeovil.

Eva's successor was a John Fowler built 0-4-2 tank locomotive, named *Nicholson*, which had been built in 1907 and was purchased from the Royal Artillery Depot in Lydd. *Nicholson* in turn lasted in service until 1934 when Dixon & Cardus went out of business.

In the meantime several changes had occurred on the tramway system. A connection had been laid from the tramway near Radcliffe Road to Mount Pleasant Wharf. Then in 1923 the connection to the main line was changed when Northam Yard was laid out, the tramway now running from No.3 siding in the yard. Day, Summers and Co. also ceased operations in 1929, but part of their site was taken over by John I Thornycroft & Co. Ltd, ship-repairers, while Pollock, Brown and Co. Ltd., scrap merchants, occupied the rest of the site.

Le Dansk took over operation of the line when Dixon & Cardus closed in 1934. They replaced *Nicholson* with a

Above: A side-on view of *Nicholson*, originally built in 1907.   (Photo: Bert Moody Collection)

four-wheeled internal combustion locomotive, which was supplied new by Muir Hill Engineering Ltd of Manchester. This locomotive was to work the line through the Second World War and into the 1950s.

SR locomotives did not work onto the line, and the line's locomotives were only allowed to cross Radcliffe Road into Northam Yard with the permission of the shunter on duty at the yard and with a flagman on duty. However, the locomotive could shunt in the yard with the permission of the shunter.

After the Second World War operation of the line was placed in the hands of Northam Joint Haulage Ltd in 1948, whose shareholders included Auguste Pellerin Ltd; Gabriel, Wade & English Ltd (Timber Merchants); and George Cohen, Sons and Co. Ltd (parent company of Pollock, Brown & Co. Ltd).

In the early 1950s the old Northam Bridge was replaced, which necessitated changing the course of the tramway. The old road crossing over Northam Bridge Road was removed, and instead the line was diverted through what was to become the Southern Independent Television studios lot, before passing under the new bridge. In addition, a temporary 3ft gauge track was laid to the west of the bridge for constructor's traffic. On the east side the old wharf was filled in and the Dixon & Cardus mill knocked down.

In 1957 the margarine factory ceased production, and the running of the line was taken over by Pollock, Brown and Co. Ltd. They provided a new locomotive, a Ruston & Hornsby four-wheel diesel mechanical, built in 1952 for another division of George Cohen. Later three Fowler 0-4-0 diesels were obtained to work on the line. No.4200002 had worked at the Royal Naval Armament depot at Dean Hill from new in 1946, arriving at Northam in 1969, No.22996, built in 1943, arrived in 1972 from RAF Chilmark, and finally No.22968, built in 1942 arrived from Hartlebury in 1974. The final locomotive to work on the line was a Hunslet 0-4-0 diesel mechanical of 1952 vintage, which was purchased from PD Fuels in 1976, having worked at Dibles Wharf just down the River Itchen (see later). All except No. 4200002, which was scrapped in 1983, lasted until the line closed in 1984.

One interesting interlude in 1978 was the brief return of steam to the line for a couple of days in the form of Peckett 0-4-0ST *Whitehead*. This was in connection with the Southern Television children's programme *The Saturday Banana*.

The end came in 1984, when BR standardised on air-braked wagons for its trains. As none of the locomotives on the line was fitted with the appropriate air-braking equipment, rail traffic ceased, and the line closed with the remaining locomotives being scrapped the following year.

Develop of the Northam Wharves Line

c.1845

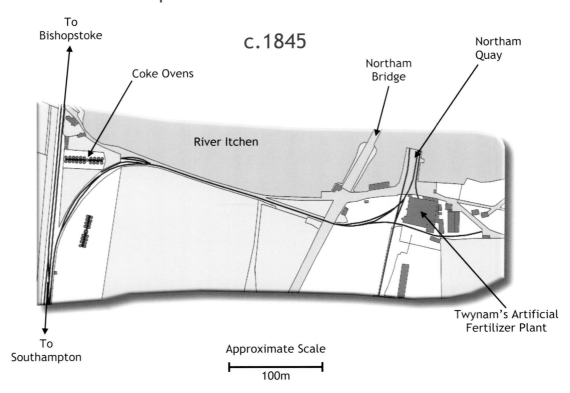

To
Bishopstoke

Coke Ovens

Northam
Bridge

Northam
Quay

River Itchen

Twynam's Artificial
Fertilizer Plant

To
Southampton

Approximate Scale

100m

c.1897

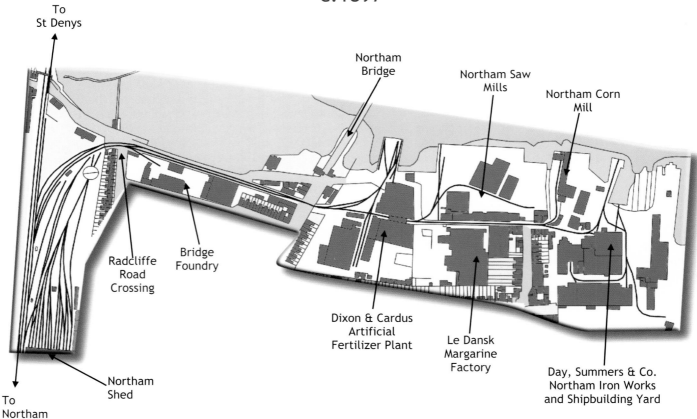

To
St Denys

Northam
Bridge

Northam Saw
Mills

Northam Corn
Mill

Radcliffe
Road
Crossing

Bridge
Foundry

Dixon & Cardus
Artificial
Fertilizer Plant

Le Dansk
Margarine
Factory

Day, Summers & Co.
Northam Iron Works
and Shipbuilding Yard

Northam
Shed

To
Northam

c.1933

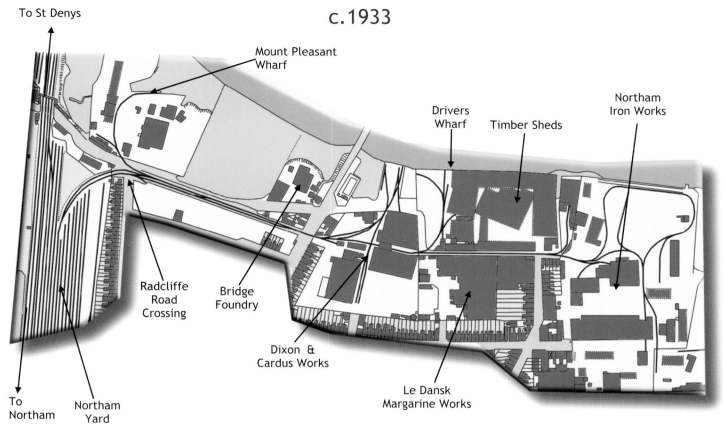

To St Denys

Mount Pleasant Wharf

Drivers Wharf

Timber Sheds

Northam Iron Works

Radcliffe Road Crossing

Bridge Foundry

To Northam

Northam Yard

Dixon & Cardus Works

Le Dansk Margarine Works

Approximate Scale

100m

c.1960

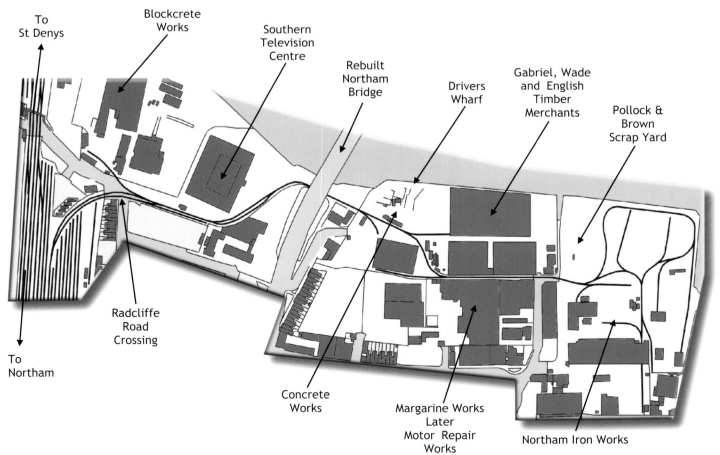

To St Denys

Blockcrete Works

Southern Television Centre

Rebuilt Northam Bridge

Drivers Wharf

Gabriel, Wade and English Timber Merchants

Pollock & Brown Scrap Yard

Radcliffe Road Crossing

To Northam

Concrete Works

Margarine Works Later Motor Repair Works

Northam Iron Works

Left: On 3rd June 1974 one of the Pollock & Brown owned Fowler 0-4-0 diesel mechanicals No.4200002 crosses Radcliffe Road on its way into Northam Yard. The 600 painted on the loco refers to the George Cohen 600 group, which was the parent company of Pollock & Brown at this time.
(Photo: R. Silsbury)

Right: Later that day the same loco is observed from the Northam Road bridge as it emerges from underneath with a train of wagons for the yard. Part of Drivers Wharf and the timber sheds can be seen above the locomotive with the *Allard* tied up at the quay.
(Photo: R. Silsbury)

Right: *Whitehead* waits in the lea of Northam Bridge before rehearsals for its role in *The Saturday Banana.* An 0-4-0ST *Whitehead* was built by Peckett in 1908 for the Cefnstylle colliery in South Wales. In 1978, when these photos were taken, *Whitehead* was based at the West Somerset Railway, and is now housed at the Midland Railway Centre, Butterley.

Left: The sharp curve can be seen that took the line across the Southern Television Centre car park. In front of the studios is the giant banana used in the children's programme in 1978.

Right: The remains of the line in January 2011 at the head of Millbank Street as the line of rails heads into the scrap yard that is still on the site.

Chapel Tramway

Above: Locomotive *Lord Fisher* is seen on the curve connecting the tramway to the main line in 1964. In the background on the left is the gasworks. (Photo: Bert Moody)

Origins

In 1843 the LSWR gave permission for a wagon turntable to be inserted in a siding at Chapel to connect to a tramway, which initially served Union, Roes and Britannia Wharves on the River Itchen. This was at the instigation of Mr E. Pritchard who had established a cement works and lime kilns on the riverside. The gasworks was also sited along the route of the tramway, but it would be many years before it was directly connected to the system.

Initially the tramway ran from the turntable across Melbourne Street and passed over what was then open land before reaching Marine Parade. Here another turntable connected with a line running north-south along Marine Parade. Directly across the turntable was a connection curving into Union Wharf, while on the northern section of line along Marine Parade there were connections to Roes Wharf and Britannia Wharf, where Pritchard's works were situated. As will be implied by the use of wagon turntables for the connections, the system was worked by horses at that time.

Over the next twenty years the area changed considerably with housing being constructed and further wharves established, while others were renamed. On the tramway a loop had been laid on the connecting line between Melbourne Street and Marine Parade alongside the now extended gasworks. Meanwhile on Marine Parade the wagon turntable had disappeared replaced by a set of points. Another loop connected with new wharves which had been built on the riverside opposite the gasworks, presumably to bring in construction material, this would later be known as Burnley Wharf. To the south Victoria and Sunderland Wharves had been built and the system developed with new facilities at Union Wharf, as well as being extended further south to connect to Baltic Wharf.

At Roes Wharf, now renamed Phoenix Wharf, a line of rails looped round the edges of the wharf jetty before re-connecting with the main line, which continued into Britannia Wharf at the northern end of the system. By now all the wagon turntables had disappeared, save for the one connecting the tramway to the LSWR, which was renewed in 1876.

Steam Power

Further developments had taken place in the system by 1897 including a link into the gasworks itself. However, it was in 1899 that the next major change occurred when J.R. Wood & Co. coal merchants, who had been based at Burnley Wharf since 1882, applied to both the LSWR and Southampton Corporation to employ steam power on the tramway. This they both agreed, with the LSWR consenting to a new connection being made to their line in January 1899.

The new connection removed the old wagon turntable but necessitated the line crossing the back gardens of a number of cottages, which had to be purchased as a result. A Peckett 0-4-0 saddle tank, built in 1884, was obtained for the line in February 1899, having been purchased secondhand from a works in South Wales. This was joined in 1902 by a new locomotive built by Andrew Barclay, which was also a 0-4-0 saddle tank. The same year the Phoenix Wharf and Coal Company was formed, and became the principle user of the system for the transportation of coal to various parts of the hinterland.

There were further changes along the wharves and additional sidings were added to the system by 1908. One significant development was the building of a conveyor from the wharf-side into the gasworks for the direct transfer of coal to the plant. However, by this time there were also significant movements of coal along the tramway to the LSWR lines for transfer to the newly opened power station by Southampton West (later Central) station.

A single road engine shed had also been built alongside Marine Parade at Burnley Wharf. In 1914 there was a change of motive power on the line, when the original Peckett was sold to a colliery in Derbyshire. It was replaced by a newly built locomotive, also a Peckett 0-4-0ST, No.1375.

The Chapel Tramway Company

When Wood & Co. moved up-river to Belvidere Wharf in June 1926 Burnley Wharf was taken over by the Southampton Gas, Light & Coke Company, who operated the gasworks. They in turn joined with the other users

the following year to form the Chapel Tramway Company Ltd and took over the running of the line.

Among the concerns involved in the new company were: Southampton Gas, Light & Coke Ltd, Hooper and Ashby Ltd (Builders Merchants), Edwin Jones & Co. Ltd (Retailers), the Cement Marketing Company, and Dolton, Bournes & Dolton Ltd (Timber and Builders Merchants). The range of companies gives an idea of the type of traffic being carried on the line at the time. This was considerable, and amounted to nearly 200,000 tons in 1928.

By 1933 the system had reached its maximum mileage, and included the provision of a new two-road locomotive shed, built on the boundary of Burnley and Victoria Wharves. There was also a second siding added in the gasworks.

At this time the tramway joined the SR at Chapel siding where there was a loop line with hand operated points, trains being able to enter or leave the loop at Chapel Road crossing to the south, or near Bevois Road Crossing to the north. At the siding there was often someone on duty to liaise with the signalman at Chapel Road by means of a bell signal, operate the points on the loop, and to be in charge of any movements from the tramway onto the siding.

The driver of a tramway locomotive was supposed to stop before crossing Melbourne Street and the flagman needed to gain permission by means of a visual signal from the person in charge at the siding, before the locomotive could enter SR property. Interestingly working instructions were issued as to how two tramway locos could work in Chapel siding, and also for SR locos to work onto the tramway.

Right: The first Andrew Barclay 0-4-0 saddle tank works No.923 spent its whole life on the tramway between 1902 and 1955. It is seen departing from Victoria Wharf past the second engine shed heading towards Marine Parade. The first wagon in its train appears to be a private owner wagon owned by Edwin Jones.
(Photographer Unknown J.R. Fairman Collection Kidderminster Railway Museum)

Development of the Chapel Tramway

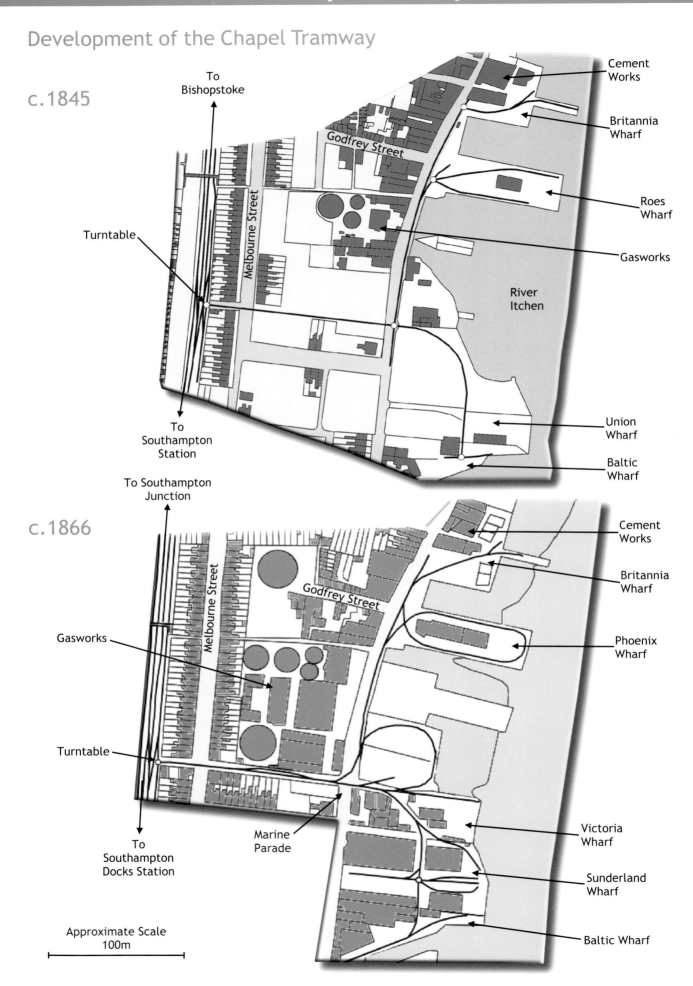

c.1845

To Bishopstoke

Godfrey Street

Turntable

Melbourne Street

To Southampton Station

Cement Works

Britannia Wharf

Roes Wharf

Gasworks

River Itchen

Union Wharf

Baltic Wharf

c.1866

To Southampton Junction

Melbourne Street

Godfrey Street

Gasworks

Turntable

To Southampton Docks Station

Marine Parade

Cement Works

Britannia Wharf

Phoenix Wharf

Victoria Wharf

Sunderland Wharf

Baltic Wharf

Approximate Scale 100m

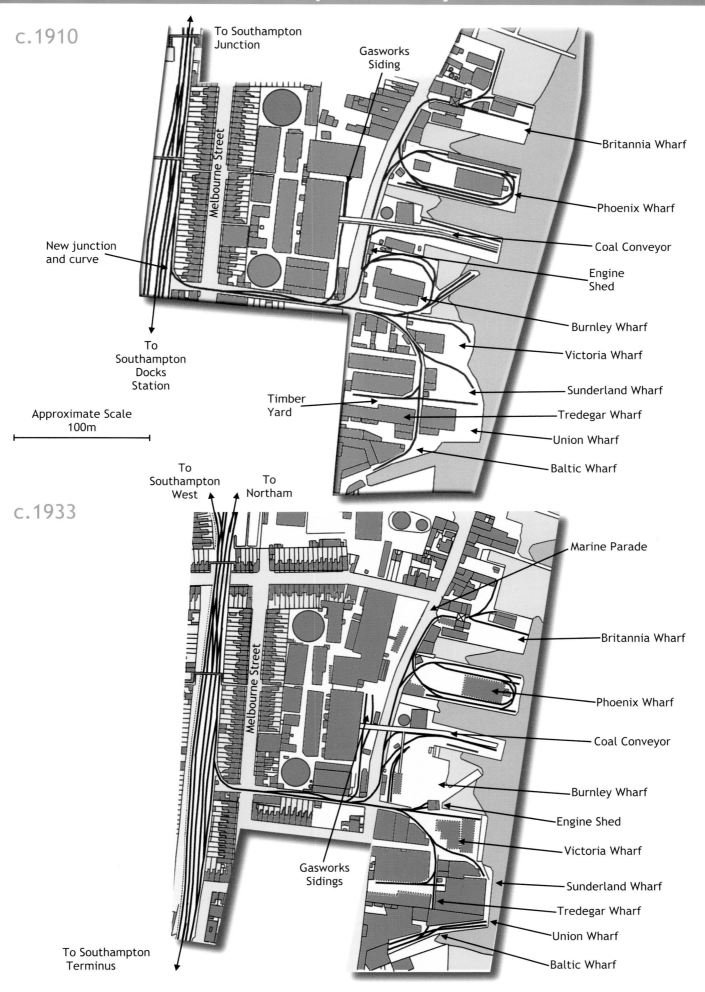

c.1910

To Southampton Junction

Gasworks Siding

New junction and curve

To Southampton Docks Station

Approximate Scale 100m

Britannia Wharf

Phoenix Wharf

Coal Conveyor

Engine Shed

Burnley Wharf

Victoria Wharf

Sunderland Wharf

Timber Yard

Tredegar Wharf

Union Wharf

Baltic Wharf

To Southampton West

To Northam

c.1933

Melbourne Street

Marine Parade

Britannia Wharf

Phoenix Wharf

Coal Conveyor

Burnley Wharf

Engine Shed

Victoria Wharf

Sunderland Wharf

Gasworks Sidings

Tredegar Wharf

Union Wharf

To Southampton Terminus

Baltic Wharf

The Second World War and Beyond

Traffic continued to develop, reaching a climax during the Second World War, although an air raid in September 1940 heavily damaged both the gasworks and tramway. Nevertheless in 1942 267,000 tons of materials were conveyed over the system.

However, during the 1950s the amount of traffic began to decline, hastened by the decline in output of coke from the gasworks as gas from Fawley refinery was piped in. Gradually the system was reduced, the connection to the gasworks was removed, and other parts of the system disconnected.

In 1955 the Andrew Barclay locomotive of 1902 was scrapped, and the tramway continued with just the single Peckett locomotive. However, in 1961 that locomotive too was replaced by another Andrew Barclay 0-4-0ST. This was of 1915 vintage, purchased from Hilsea Gasworks where it carried the name *Lord Fisher*. It became the sole source of motive power until the tramway closed.

During the 1960s traffic continued to decline, until it reached 3,106 tons in 1966, the traffic at this point consisting mainly of cement and building materials for Hooper and Ashby at Britannia Wharf. In 1967 the decision was taken to close the line, and the final train ran on 31st March 1967.

Although most remnants of the tramway have been removed a few traces remain within the wharf properties. However, substantial redevelopment of the area has led to all trace of the connection with the main line being obliterated. *Lord Fisher* has happily been preserved and is currently based at the Yeovil Steam Centre.

Aerial View of Part of the Chapel Tramway and Associated Wharves c.1924

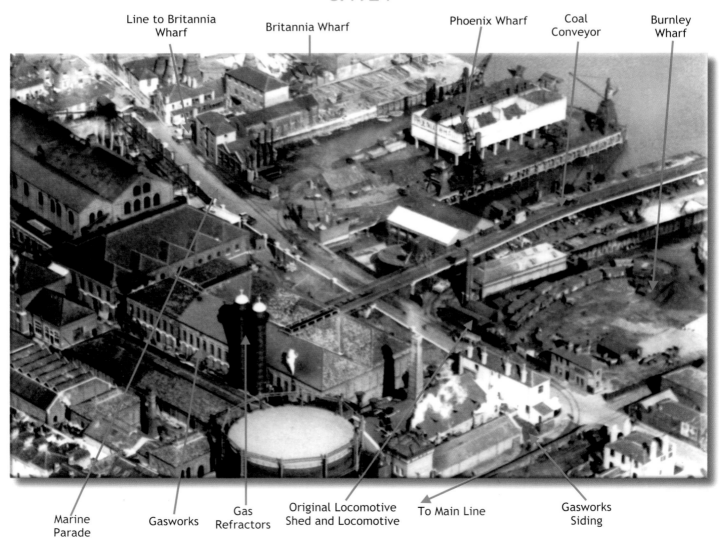

Line to Britannia Wharf — Britannia Wharf — Phoenix Wharf — Coal Conveyor — Burnley Wharf

Marine Parade — Gasworks — Gas Refractors — Original Locomotive Shed and Locomotive — To Main Line — Gasworks Siding

(Photo: J.R. Fairman Collection Kidderminster Railway Museum)

Above: Peckett No.1375 is seen outside the second engine shed on the Chapel Tramway with Burnley Wharf in the background on an unknown date. No.1375 also spent its entire working life on the tramway having been delivered new in 1914. It was finally scrapped in 1961.   (Photographer Unknown J.R. Fairman Collection Kidderminster Railway Museum)

Above: *Lord Fisher* is dwarfed by its surroundings as it runs down to Deanery to be turned on the turntable shortly after its arrival on the tramway. This was done with special permission as normally the tramway locos were not permitted on the main line. It is seen here at the southern end of the loop to which the tramway connected, the man on the ground was presumably the pointsman on duty.   (Photo: J.R. Fairman Courtesy Kidderminster Railway Museum)

Above: Looking across towards the gasworks from Britannia Wharf this photograph shows the aftermath of a bomb explosion during the Second World War. There has clearly been extensive damage. (Photo: Courtesy *Southern Daily Echo*)

Left: *Lord Fisher* was preserved and served for a number of years on the East Somerset Railway based at Cranmore. It is seen here in April 1974. By this time new nameplates had been applied.
(Photo: G.F. Bloxam Copyright P.F. Bloxam)

Left: No trace of the route the tramway took from Marine Parade to the main line remains in March 2011.

Right: Looking along the course of the tramway across Marine Parade and into Victoria Wharf in March 2011. The second locomotive shed was probably just to the left of the pile of sand in the distance.

Left: Some of the original tracks can just be made out on Burnley Wharf in March 2011. The original locomotive shed was probably at the far end of the office building.

Eling Tramway

Above: Manning Wardle 0-4-0 saddle tank *Cameronian* built in 1877 came to Eling in 1923, working there until 1950. It is seen here on the quayside by the River Test In May 1947.   (Photo: Harry Townley Copyright Industrial Railway Society)

For centuries Eling creek was a centre for industry, with a mill being first mentioned there in the Doomsday book. This was rebuilt several times with the current mill dating from the 1770s.

Nearby, Eling Wharf had for many years served as the port for Salisbury and the New Forest. By the mid-nineteenth century the land was owned by Sir John Barker Mill, and leased to a number of tenants, including the Mumford Steam Mill which produced fertilizer, and John Bull, a coal merchant. There was also a corn store and timber merchants. Trade was significant, and John Bull stated that in 1846 over 6,000 tons of coal had been landed at his wharf frontage alone.

The development of the railways, as well as the docks and Town Quay area in Southampton, were having an effect on trade from the wharf. So when the Southampton and Dorchester Railway was promoted lobbying took place for a branch from the proposed main line. As a result in 1845 permission was given for a survey for such a line.

This led to a route being submitted as part of a Bill on behalf of the S&DR in 1847, which also included a proposed branch to Lymington. It branched from the main line near the site of the current Totton station, and then crossed the Lyndhurst turnpike on the level before running on a straight course to the wharf half a mile distant. However, the route was not without controversy,

which led to an enquiry being held on behalf of the Admiralty in Southampton in February 1847. Here an alternative route was proposed by a Mr Sharland, who was a tenant of one of Sir John's other wharves at Redbridge, which would have been much more favourable to himself.

In the end the original route prevailed and it was formally authorised as part of the Southampton and Dorchester Railway Act on 2nd July 1847 as the Eling Branch Railway. However, it was not to be until 1851 that agreement was reached between Sir John and the LSWR which enabled the branch to be built. Under the agreement the LSWR built a connection from the main line to their boundary at the edge of the turnpike, from where Sir John completed the line to the wharf. The line was apparently ready for traffic in late 1851.

Originally at the wharf the line essentially split into three, one line running straight on to the quay at the creek-side, while one branch ran to the west to the steam mill, and another to the east to serve a quay on the River Test. By 1866 another line intersected the branch at right angles a way back from the creek to serve a wood preserving and pitch works, and another quay on the Test.

Sir John Barker Mill's estate passed to his widow on his death in February 1860, and upon her death to his third cousin Mrs Marianne Vaudrey. During this time the line continued to operate and the LSWR used it for the

Above: The second locomotive purchased by Burt, Boulton & Haywood for work on the wharf in 1923, was another 0-4-0ST named *Benton*, which had been built by Black, Hawthorn and Co. in 1896. It is seen here in May 1947.

(Photo: Harry Townley Copyright Industrial Railway Society)

delivery of permanent way supplies. While it was horse-worked for most of its length, LSWR locomotives were also known to venture across the main road onto the branch. This is testified to by a discussion as to whether the LSWR should be called upon to erect gates at the crossing, held by the New Forest Board of Guardians, and reported in the *Hampshire Advertiser* in June 1882.

Here the LSWR stated that a locomotive only ventured across the road twice a month, unless a load of sleepers had been unloaded at the wharf. In the end the board did not call for the erection of gates, partly as they were uncertain as to whose responsibility it was, the LSWR's, or Mrs Vaudrey, but instead opted to call on the company to provide a man with a red flag. Of course the fact that the LSWR acquired Redbridge Wharf in 1881, and established their permanent way works there, also probably had an impact by reducing some of the freight passing through the wharf.

This uncertainty as to responsibilities seems, in part, due to the fact that apparently there was no operating agreement in place for the branch, a situation rectified on 22nd October 1886, when an agreement was signed with Mrs Vaudrey leasing the LSWR's line to her for 999 years. Part of this agreement also stated that if the line on the wharf fell into disuse for three years then the LSWR had the right to sever the connection, a power that would be used just over a hundred years later.

By the end of the century a second line of rails had been laid alongside the main branch to form a run-round loop almost from the road crossing to the wharf. This appears to have become three sets of lines forming two loops by 1910. At the wharf a wagon turntable had been installed giving access to a line running along the wharf edge down towards the tide mill. At the north-east corner of the wharf site, the creosoting plant had been extended by 1910 to include a tar distillery.

The line continued to be used through the First World War, and was even going to be used by the Admiralty until the end of the conflict intervened. Then in the early 1920s extensive use was made of the facilities at Eling in connection with the construction of Fawley Refinery. Over 5,000 tons of construction materials for the refinery passed through the wharf, and for a few months when production started some oil products were shipped via Eling.

A major change occurred in 1923 when the firm of Burt, Boulton & Haywood took over the lease. They had many interests on a number of sites, including owning the Regent petrol brand, but seem to have used Eling for timber, and agricultural products. During the 1920s the wharf system was extended with extra loops and sidings laid out.

They also acquired two steam locomotives both 0-4-0 saddle tanks. The first, *Cameronian*, was built by Manning

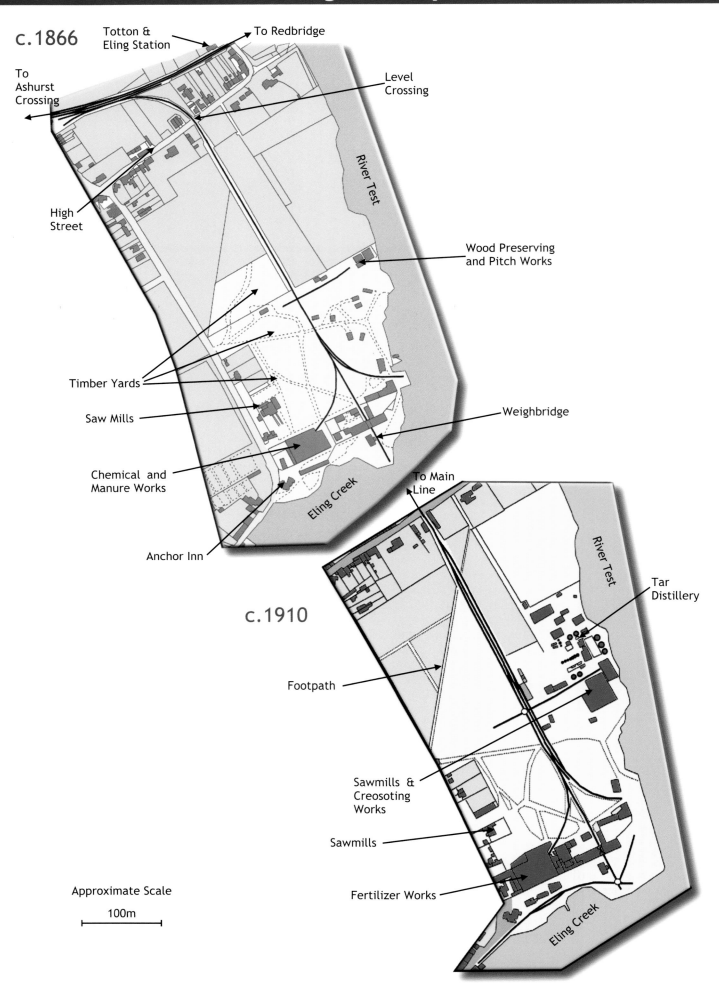

c.1866

Totton &
Eling Station

To Redbridge

To
Ashurst
Crossing

Level
Crossing

River Test

High
Street

Wood Preserving
and Pitch Works

Timber Yards

Saw Mills

Weighbridge

Chemical and
Manure Works

To Main
Line

Anchor Inn

Eling Creek

c.1910

River Test

Tar
Distillery

Footpath

Sawmills &
Creosoting
Works

Sawmills

Fertilizer Works

Eling Creek

Approximate Scale

100m

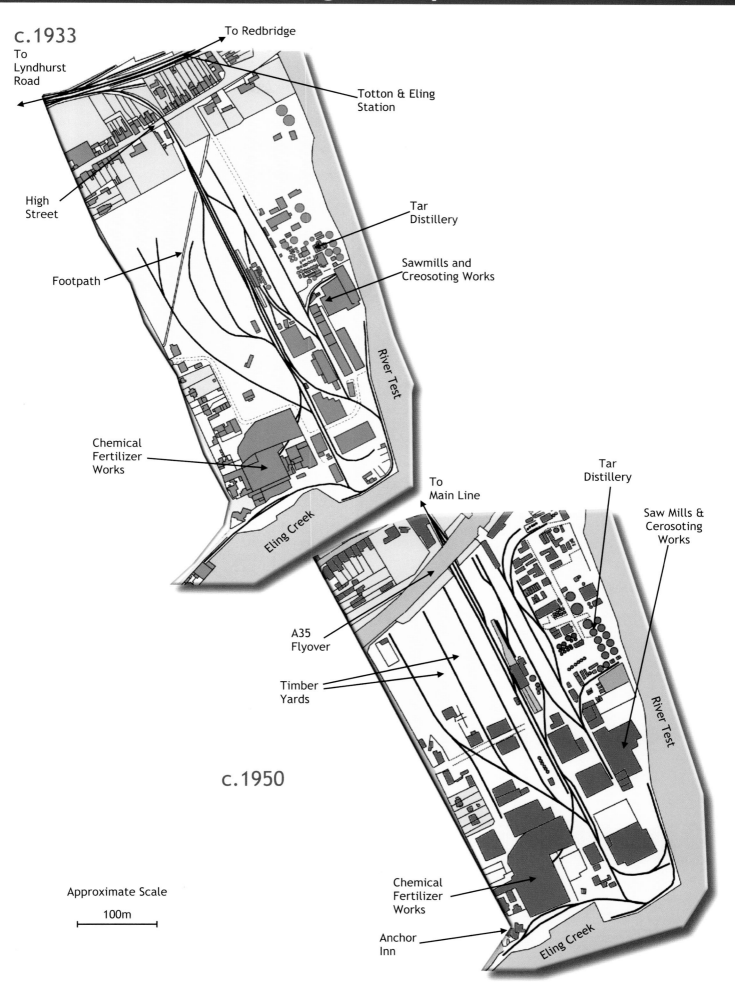

c.1933

To Lyndhurst Road

To Redbridge

Totton & Eling Station

Tar Distillery

Sawmills and Creosoting Works

High Street

Footpath

River Test

Chemical Fertilizer Works

Eling Creek

To Main Line

Tar Distillery

Saw Mills & Cerosoting Works

A35 Flyover

Timber Yards

River Test

c.1950

Approximate Scale

100m

Chemical Fertilizer Works

Anchor Inn

Eling Creek

Wardle in 1877 and came to Eling from the Air Ministry at Halton in Buckinghamshire. Meanwhile the second was *Benton*, built by Black, Hawthorn & Co. in 1896, and was purchased from the Ministry of Munitions Rolling Mill at Woolston, where there was a small rail system leading out onto a jetty.

At this time the principal firms operating at Eling aside from Burt, Boulton & Haywood, were South Western Tar Distilleries, who in 1931 were the largest users of the branch, James Fletcher and Son, sawmill, and Spooner & Bailey, who ran a bone crushing business for the fertilizer industry. In 1935 crossing gates were finally installed across the A35.

During the Second World War the wharf suffered from several air raids one of which, on 26th March 1941, resulted in a major explosion and fire. After the war Fisons built a new fertilizer plant at the wharf, and the layout of the sidings was changed, the work being carried out by the SR.

April 1948 saw the purchase of another locomotive. *Benton II* was an 0-4-0 saddle tank built by Andrew Barclay in 1912, and originally supplied to Babcock & Wilcox in Renfrewshire. It came to replace both of the original locomotives which were scrapped by 1950. The 1950s also saw a major change to the landscape near the road crossing with the opening of the A35 flyover, which passed over the wharf line offering road users a fleeting look at the wharf lines as they went by.

Traffic continued through the 1950s and 60s. In November 1963, for example, 142 loaded wagons arrived on the branch and 79 departed. However, in 1966 *Benton II* was scrapped to be replaced by a Ruston & Hornsby four-wheeled shunter originally built in 1942.

The 1970s saw the opening of an ARC roadstone processing plant on the wharf, with a new siding being laid to it. This brought main line diesels onto the branch, and class 33, 47 and 56 diesels could be occasionally seen working trains on it. In 1975 the Ruston diesel was sold, any shunting being done by the steam cranes that operated on the site.

A new siding was inaugurated for a Redland tiles depot in 1988. However, the same year the ARC Roadstone workings ceased. In 1989 Burt, Boulton & Haywood was taken over by Travis Perkins, and the following year the Redland workings ended. The tramway then lay dormant for three years until the clause in the original lease was invoked and the connection to the main line severed, thus ending nearly 140 years of rail activity. Today the wharf still serves as an industrial estate, and until 2012 the crossing gates remained in-situ at the road crossing, but these have now been removed.

Left: One of the South Western Tar Distilleries tank wagons when new. (Photo: HMRS Hurst Nelson Collection)

Above: The scene at Eling Wharf on 28th August 1968 as Ken Carr looked down from the A35 flyover. One of the steam cranes can be seen in operation in the middle distance. The large building in the centre-right background has a roof sign proclaiming it is home to Burt, Boulton & Haywood.

Right: On the same day this is the view from the other side of the flyover looking towards Totton station showing the curve round to the road crossing from the main line. One of the platform nameboards can be seen to the right of the former mill building in the background.

(Both Photos: K.G. Carr Copyright P. Fidczuk)

Left: At the crossing gates on 17th February 1989 a gathering anticipates the arrival of a train.
(Photo: John H. Bird Copyright Southern-Images)

Left: The gates are opened as class 47 No.47123 creeps around the curve with a freight from Eastleigh.
(All photos this page: John H. Bird Copyright Southern-Images)

Right: Photographed from the flyover No.47123 runs round its train for Redland tiles.

Left: Having passed under the flyover the points are being changed to allow No.47123 back onto its wagons so that it can propel them down into the appropriate siding.

Left: On 13th January 1988 No.47016 *The Tolman Group* arrives at Eling Wharf with two wagons of tiles to mark the opening of the Redland depot.
(Photo: R. Silsbury)

Above: The crossing gates are still in place across the old track-bed in January 2011 with the bridge under the flyover leading onto the wharf in the background. Just over a year later they would be gone.

Left: The remains of *Benton II* presumably rescued when it was scrapped at the wharf in 1966, and subsequently used as a plantholder at a house in Totton until it was re-discovered. It is now on display at the Totton & Eling Heritage Centre near Eling Tidal Mill.

Bull's Run

Above: Ex-docks class B4 shunter *Corrall Queen*, formerly *Normandy*, at Dibles Wharf on an unknown date in 1968-69 still carrying its BR numberplate. On the left the front of locomotive *Bonnie Prince Charlie* can be seen. The cab roof on *Corrall Queen* was modified as seen here sometime during April and May 1968. (Photographer Unknown)

Joseph Bull & Sons were well known builders in the Southampton area as well as many other places, and were responsible for constructing many of the railway structures in the area. However, they were also responsible for buildings such as the Winchester Guildhall and the Royal Courts of Justice in London. They had a works at Belvidere Wharf at Northam, and in the early 1860s applied for a connection to be made between there and the main line just north of Northam Junction. This the LSWR consented to, and so Bull's Run siding, as it became known, was laid and in operation by 1866.

Originally the siding consisted of a single track which ran behind Northam Junction signal box, and under the Northam Bridge Road overbridge, before curving down to the river. At this time much of this land was not built up. When the track reached Britannia Road it divided, with the one line running across Britannia Road and then crossing Belvidere Road, before reaching the Bull Co.'s workshop on Belvidere Wharf. Meanwhile the second branch ran south-east along Britannia Road, before curving east and itself crossing Belvidere Road to the wharf where Summers & Payne had their yacht building business.

By 1900 Bull's had moved out of the workshop and the wharf was subsequently occupied by the Powell Duffryn

Steam Coal Company, which had been originally founded in South Wales in 1864. One of the mysteries of these early days is to whether the line was worked by horses or by LSWR locomotives. It is possible that it was the latter, and certainly there is a record of a working agreement with the LSWR for the siding in 1904.

Part of this working agreement possibly led to the doubling of the majority of the line from Northam, where expansion of the goods yard had led to alterations in the line of the siding to Belvidere Road. It is also likely that when this was done the southerly line was removed. However, between 1912 and 1917 there was a lengthy dispute between the LSWR and the owners which eventually had to go to arbitration.

During World War One the Admiralty made extensive use of Belvidere Wharf for the delivery of coal, and much of this passed over the tramway. But after the war the line fell into relative disuse until it was sold in March 1924 to Thomas Gater, Bradfield & Co. whose tenants were the National Benzole Company Ltd. Thomas Gater, Bradfield & Co. agreed to pay the SR £265 towards the reconstruction of the siding, and £12 per annum for maintenance of the connection at Northam. A new user arrived in 1926 when J.R. Wood & Co., the coal merchants, moved into the Belvidere shipyard, formerly

Above: Peckett 0-4-0 saddle tank *Bristol* at the head of a train from Northam Yard crossing Britannia Road on 16th September 1953. The lifting mechanism for the section of fence which acts as a gate is worth noting. (Photo K.G. Carr Copyright P. Fidczuk)

occupied by James Dible and Sons, from their old base at Burnley Wharf further down river (see page 131).

They made a new connection to the original siding into Dibles Wharf, with associated sidings to the wharf-side. In addition, they also acquired the locomotive *Bretwalda* from the SR in 1926, which was now surplus to requirements. *Bretwalda* served the line for nine years until replaced in 1935 by an 0-4-0 saddle tank, built by Peckett in 1923 for the Barnsley Gas Company named *Bristol*.

Working instructions for the line in 1934 were that wagons to go to the wharves were to be placed on the north line at Northam ready for collection by the tramway engine, while outgoing wagons were left on the south road. Interestingly in contrast to the instructions for the Northam Wharves and Chapel lines, Tramway locos were not allowed to work into the yard at Northam. A further restriction was that wagons of a longer wheelbase than 12ft were banned from the line.

In February 1940 ownership of Dibles Wharf passed to Southern Wharves Ltd, and by the 1950s not only had the system been slightly extended within the wharf site, but also in 1952 a second locomotive was delivered. This was a brand-new Peckett 0-4-0ST works No.2128, which never carried a name.

Once again ownership of the wharf changed, passing to P.D.Fuels (Corralls) Ltd in October 1962. *Bristol* was scrapped, and replaced by another former docks locomotive in December 1963 when ex-BR No. 30096, originally ex-LSWR No.96 *Normandy*, arrived on the line. Upon arrival at Dibles Wharf it was renamed *Corrall Queen*. It was destined to probably become the most famous locomotive in Southampton.

By 1967 Dibles Wharf had become a major distribution depot for the area. Coal was brought in by road, rail and sea, with over 90,000 tons of coal and other fuels handled there annually. Peckett No.2128 was sold for scrap in 1965, and replaced by a Robert Stephenson & Hawthorn-built 0-4-0 saddle tank *Bonnie Prince*

Left: The same scene as above in March 2011.

Left: Peckett 0-4-0 saddle tank, works No.2128, which arrived new on the line in 1952 is photographed on the wharf on 5th May 1960.
(Photo: R.K. Blencowe Collection)

Charlie. This had originally worked at Hamworthy Quay having been supplied there from new in 1949. However, it proved lacking in power and only lasted at the wharf until 1969, when it was purchased by the Salisbury Steam Trust and is now based at the Didcot Railway Centre.

Meantime diesel power had arrived at Dibles Wharf in the form of a Baguley 0-4-0 diesel mechanical locomotive No.3568 in February 1968, having previously worked at Bass, Mitchell & Butlers Brewery in Burton-upon-Trent from new in 1961. Numbered PD No.1 it was to last at the wharf until the end of rail operations. It was joined in 1971 by Hunslet 0-4-0DM No.4262 built in 1952, which had formerly served at Portsmouth Dockyard.

In 1972 steam operations at Dibles Wharf came to an end, but it was a happy ending, as *Corrall Queen* was sold to the Bulleid Preservation Society and moved to the Bluebell Railway where it is still based today. Diesel No.4262 lasted until 1976 when it was sold to Pollock, Brown and Co. at Northam Iron works. Its replacement was an 0-6-0 diesel mechanical locomotive built by Hudswell Clarke in 1962, and acquired from the Manchester Ship Canal in 1975. It was destined to become the last locomotive to operate on the line.

With the decline in the domestic fuel market in the 1970s and 80s it was eventually decided to cease fuel operations at Dibles Wharf in 1987. Instead Corralls transferred their depot to Totton Goods Yard and the Bull's Run siding went out of use, with the connection to Northam Yard being removed in 1989. The two remaining diesel locomotives were moved just up the river to the Haydon Bailey Private Museum established at James Wharf, but both were eventually scrapped in March 1991. Thus ended the wharf lines on the River Itchen.

Left: *Corrall Queen* and *Bonnie Prince Charlie* at Dibles Wharf in January 1969 shortly before the latter was purchased by the Salisbury Steam Trust.
(Photo: John H. Bird Copyright Southern-Images)

Left: *Corrall Queen* heads across Belvidere Road into Dibles Wharf with a train of wagons c.1964.
(All Photos this page: M.R. Wilkins Copyright E. Brack)

Right: Looking south along Belvidere Road as *Corrall Queen* crosses again c.1964.

Left: *Corrall Queen* takes water on Dibles Wharf c.1964. In the loco shed in the background Peckett tank No.2128 can just be seen.

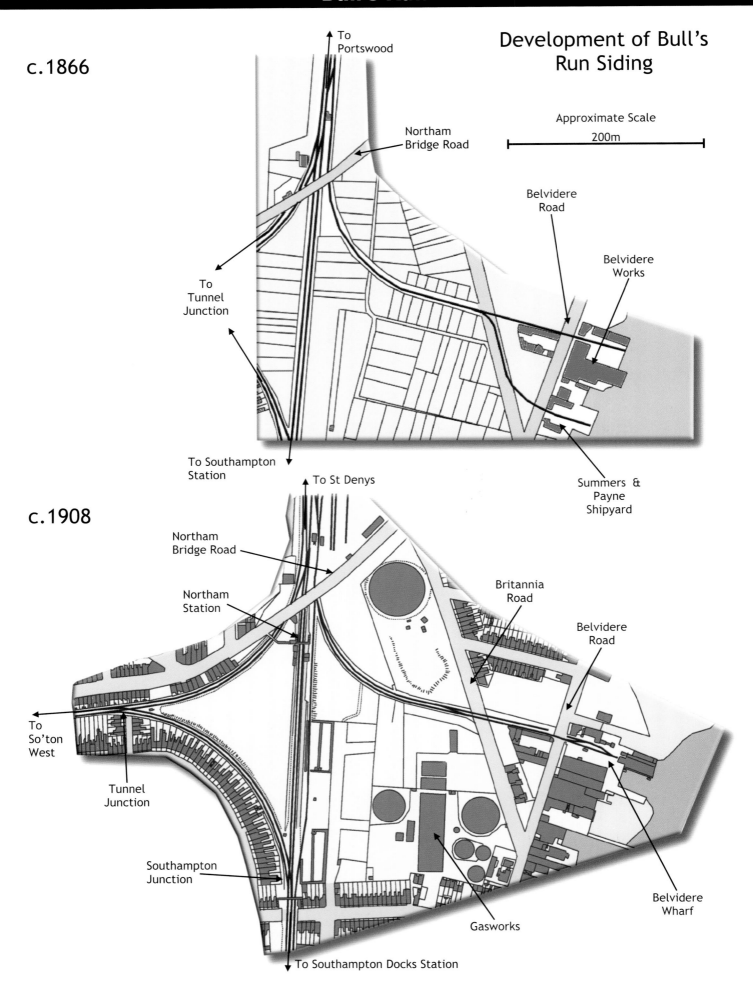

Development of Bull's Run Siding

c.1866

To Portswood

Northam Bridge Road

Approximate Scale
200m

Belvidere Road

Belvidere Works

To Tunnel Junction

Summers & Payne Shipyard

To Southampton Station

c.1908

To St Denys

Northam Bridge Road

Northam Station

Britannia Road

Belvidere Road

To So'ton West

Tunnel Junction

Southampton Junction

Gasworks

Belvidere Wharf

To Southampton Docks Station

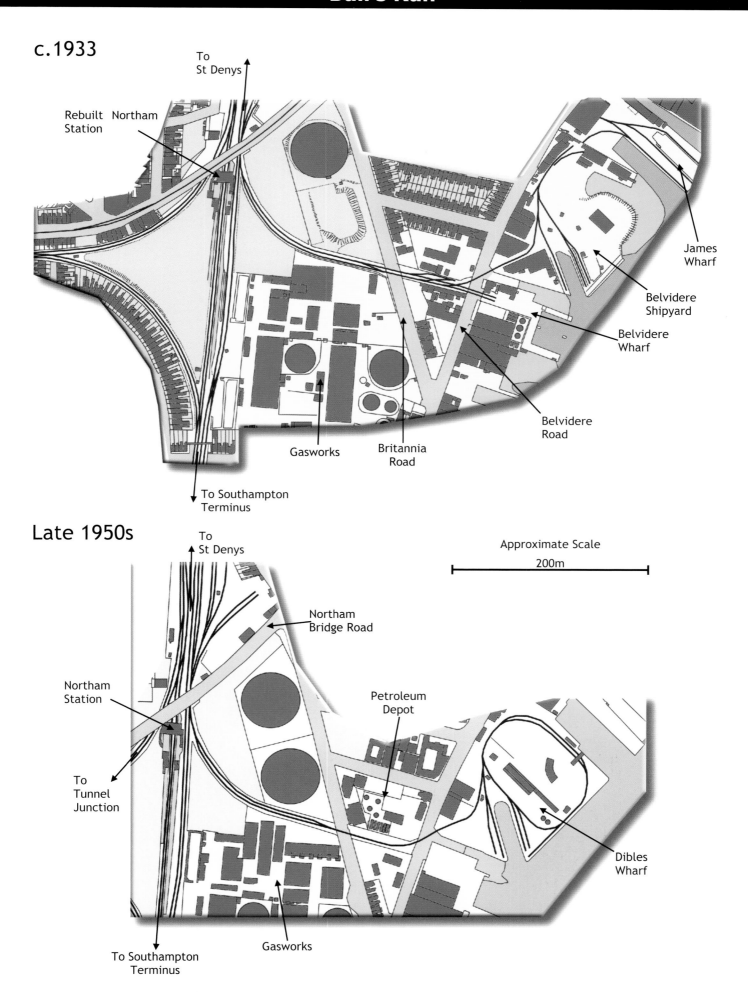

c.1933

To St Denys

Rebuilt Station   Northam

James Wharf

Belvidere Shipyard

Belvidere Wharf

Belvidere Road

Gasworks

Britannia Road

To Southampton Terminus

Late 1950s

Approximate Scale
200m

To St Denys

Northam Bridge Road

Northam Station

Petroleum Depot

To Tunnel Junction

Dibles Wharf

To Southampton Terminus

Gasworks

Left and Below: *Corrall Queen* next to the makeshift engine shed on Dibles Wharf in April 1968.

(Photos: T. Hastings)

Left: Baguley 0-4-0 diesel mechanical locomotive No. 3568 had previously worked at Bass, Mitchell and Butlers Brewery in Burton-upon-Trent from new in 1961 before arriving at Dibles Wharf in February 1968. It is seen here at the head of a train of wagons unloading coal on the wharf in July 1968.

(Photo: John H. Bird Copyright Southern-Images)

Left: The Baguley retained its brown Bass livery and number at Dibles Wharf for some time, as seen here in July 1968.

(Photo: John H. Bird Copyright Southern-Images)

Right: After rail operations ceased on the wharf the two remaining diesels were retained for a time before being moved to a private museum on James Wharf. They were finally scrapped in 1991. Here the last locomotive to work on the line, the Hudswell Clarke 0-6-0, built in 1962 is seen out of service at Dibles Wharf on 2nd May 1990.

(Photo: R. Silsbury)

Left: The Baguley 0-4-0 in its final livery is also photographed at the wharf on the same day. (Photo: R. Silsbury)

Left: Happily unlike the diesels the final two steam locomotives to work at Dibles Wharf are preserved. *Corrall Queen* is at the Bluebell Railway, while *Bonnie Prince Charlie* is based at the Didcot Steam Centre. The photograph on the left shows it at Didcot in the early days of the centre.

(Photographer Unknown)

Right: In June 1994 to celebrate the 50th Anniversary of the D-Day landings No.30096, now rebuilt in its early 20th century condition as LSWR No.96 *Normandy*, made a return to Southampton Docks. It is seen here in rather damp conditions.

(Photographer Unknown)

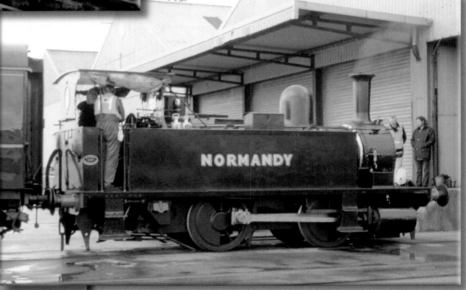

Left: The course of the Bull's Run siding between Britannia and Belvidere Roads in March 2011.

Right: The entrance to the former Dibles Wharf in March 2011.

Power Station

Above: A posed shot with probably newly arrived Baguley-built locomotive No.2 on the exchange sidings. This loco was delivered in 1931, the date of the photo probably being confirmed by the absence of the Civic Centre in the background which would have been under construction in the early 1930s. Note the angle of the traction pole on the locomotive indicating that the locomotive is on a non-wired road, the track in the centre being the line to the power station.   (Photo: Courtesy Bert Moody Collection)

Southampton's first electric generating station was opened by the Southampton Electric Light and Power Company in the street known as Back of the Walls in 1888, supplying the first electric street lights in the town the following year. In 1896 Southampton Corporation bought the company and not long after began to plan for a new power station. This would be built on reclaimed land on the shore line between Southampton West and the tunnel entrance on the other side of Western Shore Road (later Western Esplanade). It would serve the requirements of the rapidly expanding street lighting and new electric tramway system, as well as the needs of individual households.

Work on the new site began in 1902 and in May that year it was reported that the LSWR was prepared to lay down a siding from their line to their boundary for £40, or an annual rental of £4. This was agreed by the Corporation, and they started work to construct the line from the LSWR across the road into the power station site. However, a Mr Hill objected to the construction of the crossing across the road. Therefore, there then followed a discussion with the Board of Trade as to whether the Corporation needed authority to build the crossing.

Originally the Corporation argued that the line was only to be worked by horses, and the crossing would only be used early in the morning or late at night to bring construction materials onto the site, mainly filling material obtained from the building of the Trafalgar Dry Dock. However, it does need to be noted that at the same time an unsuccessful search was going on for a 'mobile steam locomotive crane', so maybe there was a slight economy with the truth!

The necessary authority was granted in October 1903, by which time agreement had been reached with the LSWR that the siding would be worked by 550V d.c. electric overhead equipment. Eight poles for the overhead could then be erected on the railway company's land. At the same time it was agreed that a suitable 0-4-0 locomotive would be built in the Corporation tramway workshops at a cost of £146 8s 5d.

In 1904 the new power station began generating electricity, and on 16th December the connections passed Board of Trade inspection, with a 4mph speed limit, meaning the new locomotive was brought into use. The cost of the siding construction was said to have been £112 2s 3d, while the Board of Trade certificate cost £78 15s, and the overhead equipment £72 16s 1d. Now the siding was used to supply coal to the power station. This was transported to the exchange siding from the wharves at Marine Parade via the Chapel Tramway. A tender for two

Development of the Power Station Line

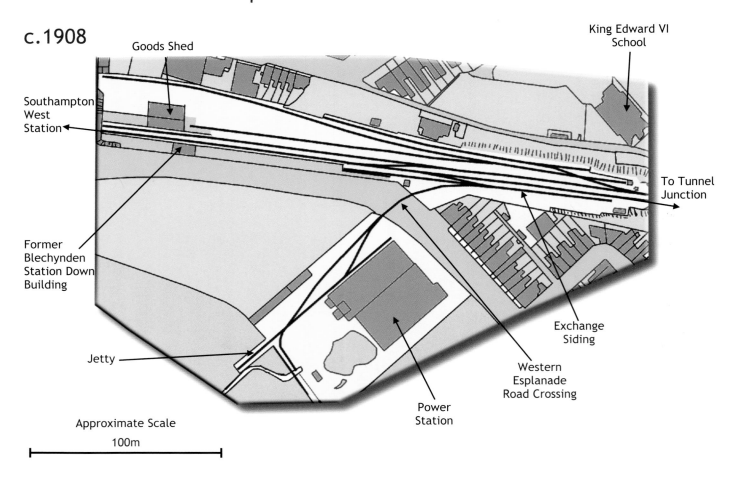

c.1908

King Edward VI School

Goods Shed

Southampton West Station

Former Blechynden Station Down Building

Jetty

Approximate Scale
100m

Power Station

Western Esplanade Road Crossing

Exchange Siding

To Tunnel Junction

ten ton wagons for this work was sought in February 1905.

Initially the line consisted of just a single track into the site, with a loop, which then led to a short jetty, and two short sidings. However, the facilities started to prove inadequate, particularly during the First World War, and in December 1916 it was stated that further sidings were required. This was reinforced when in March 1917 a bill for £27 15s arrived from the LSWR for the storage of trucks in their sidings beyond the agreed period. At this time it was said that eight to ten trucks of coal were required every day in winter, and siding accommodation for up to forty trucks was needed, but nothing seems to have happened.

After the war another possibility was discussed, that of using the old train ferry line and jetty to receive coal supplies, as well as providing additional siding space. Again, though, nothing came of the plan.

During the 1920s the power station was enlarged, and by 1933 the rail system had also had been re-laid with additional capacity. Of course by this time too the power station was no longer on the water's edge due to the reclamation process that had been going in connection with the docks extension. Now the power station was

entirely landlocked. The enlarged station also required larger qualities of coal, and so in 1931 an additional 0-4-0 locomotive was purchased from Baguley at a cost of £1,139.

Traffic, though, continued to increase with fifty wagon loads of coal passing over the lines daily by 1939. Therefore, a third locomotive was obtained from Greenwood & Batley. Increased demand also led to the extension of the rail system, and by the end of the war the system had reached its zenith.

However, after the cessation of hostilities, and the nationalisation of the electricity industry, there was a switch from rail to road for the conveyance of coal from Dibles Wharf to the power station, and the connection with the main line fell into disuse. Locomotive No.1 was scrapped in 1953, and Nos. 2 & 3 in 1960. Finally the connection to the mainline was lifted in 1964.

The power station itself was closed and demolished in 1977, although part of the site is now used for Southampton's Geo-Thermal power station. This utilises water pumped through the hot layers of rock beneath the city to create heat, and in turn create electricity. Part of the plant's output now also supplies the docks.

c.1933

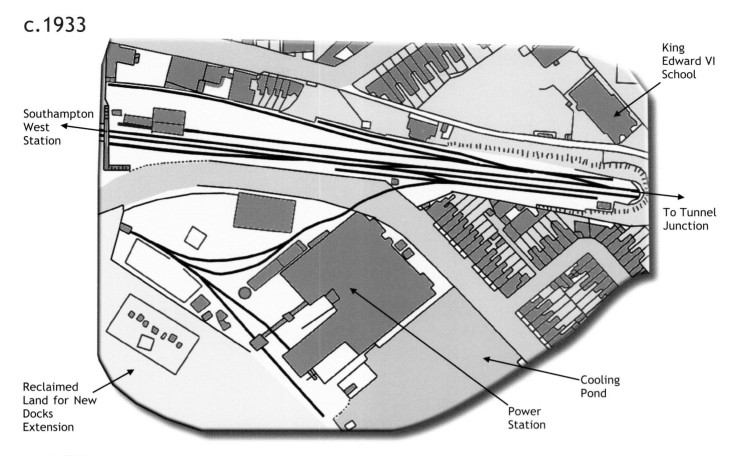

Southampton West Station

King Edward VI School

To Tunnel Junction

Reclaimed Land for New Docks Extension

Cooling Pond

Power Station

c.1950

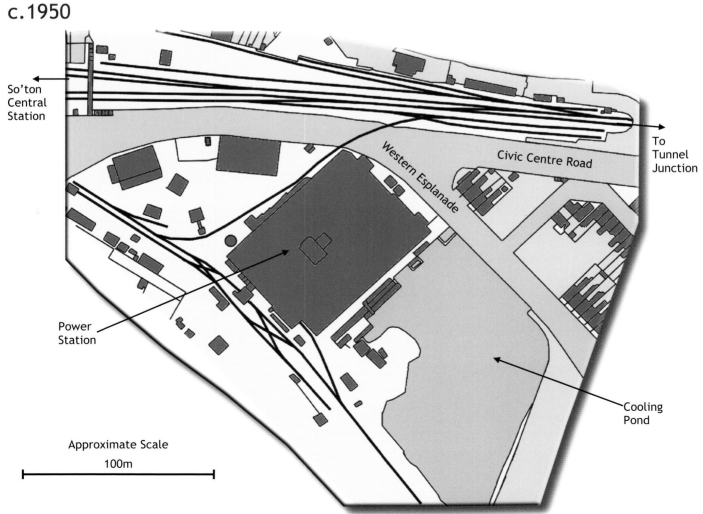

So'ton Central Station

Western Esplanade

Civic Centre Road

To Tunnel Junction

Power Station

Cooling Pond

Approximate Scale

100m

Top: Locomotive No.1 built in the Corporation's Tramway workshops in 1904 is seen in the yard at the power station on 3rd August 1950. The clock tower of Southampton Central station can be seen in the background.   (Photo: Courtesy John Bailey/Bert Moody Collection)

Middle: Locomotive No.2 in the yard at the power station on an unknown date. In the centre background locomotive No.3 built by Greenwood & Batley in 1939 can just be seen. No.2 can also be glimpsed on the right of the lower photograph on page 86 of *Southern Rails Around Southampton*.   (Photographer Unknown)

Left: On 12th April 1952 locomotive No.1 is seen out of service by the cooling pond in the south-east corner of the power station site awaiting scrapping.   (Photo: Copyright Railphotoprints)

Bibliography

Books

150 Years of Southampton Docks, B. Moody, Kingfisher Railway Productions, 1988
A Further Look at Southampton's Quayside Railways, D. Marden, Kestrel Railway Books, 2009
A Souvenir of Southampton Docks, Southern Railway, 1930
An Illustrated History of Southern Wagons Volumes One & Four, G. Bixley, A. Blackburn, R. Chorley, M. King, J. Newton (Vol.1), OPC,1984 & 2002
Castleman's Corkscrew Volumes 1&2, B.L. Jackson, Oakwood Press, 2007 & 2008
Docks and Ports: 1 Southampton, D.L. Williams, Ian Allan, 1984
History of the Southern Railway, C.F. Dendy Marshall Revised R.W. Kidner, Ian Allan, 1963 & 1982
Hospital Ships and Ambulance Trains, J.H. Plumridge, Seeley, Service & Co., 1975
Locomotives of the London and South Western Railway, Volumes 1&2, D.L. Bradley, Railway Correspondence and Travel Society, 1965, 1967
LNWR Great War Ambulance Trains, P.A. Millard, LNWR Society, 1993
LSWR Carriages Volume One, G.R. Weddell, Wild Swan Publications, 1992
LSWR Carriages in the Twentieth Century, G.R. Weddell, OPC, 2001
LSWR Carriages Volumes Three and Four, G.R. Weddell, Kestrel Books, 2005 & 2006
Netley Hospital and Its Railways, J.R. Fairman, Kingfisher Railway Productions, 1984
Southampton Docks Centenary, Southern Railway, 1938
Southampton Docks Handbook of Rates, Charges and General Information, Southern Railway, 1926, 1927, 1938, 1947
Southampton Docks Handbook of Rates, Charges and General Information, British Transport Commission Docks Division, 1960
Southampton Docks Official Sailing List and Shipping Guide, Southern Railway, March 1928
Southampton Gateway to the World, A. Arnott, The History Press, 2010
Southampton Shipping Guide, British Transport Docks Board, 1971
Southampton's Quayside Steam, D. Marden, Kestrel Railway Books, 2007
Southampton's Railways, B. Moody, Atlantic Publishers, 1992, 1997
Southern Titled Trains, D.W. Winkworth, David & Charles, 1988
Special Instructions relative to the Working Of Traffic into and out of Southampton Docks and over the Dock Lines, British Transport Commission, 1958
The B4 Dock Tanks, P. Cooper, Kingfisher Railway Productions, 1988
The London and South Western Railway Volumes 1&2, R.A. Williams, David & Charles, 1968, 1973
The LSWR in the Twentieth Century, J.N. Faulkner & R.A. Williams, David & Charles, 1988
The Story of Southampton Docks, M. Roussel, Breedon Books, 2009
The Story of the Southern USA Tanks, H. Sprenger, K. Robertson and C. Sprenger, KRB Publications, 2004

Magazine and Journal Articles

Ambulance Trains on the Lancashire and Yorkshire Railway, A. Earnshaw, *Backtrack* November/December 1992
Of Inestimable Value: The Train Ferries at Southampton, F. Neill, *The South Western Circular* July, October 2005
Port Lines: Southampton Docks and their Railways, D. Thrower, *Steam World* January, February, March 2002
Special Traffic- The Waterloo to Southampton Docks 'Ocean Liner Expresses', M. Harris, *Steam Days* October 1997
Railway Ports - Southampton, J.F. Clarke, *The Railway Magazine*, March, April, May 1909
Plus various editions of *British Railways Magazine*, *Southern Railway Magazine*, and *The Railway Magazine*.

Primary resources consulted include:
British Library Newspaper Archive
LSWR Minute Books
SDC Minute Books
SR Minute Books
British Transport Commission Minute Books
Railway Executive Committee Minute Books
Various records at the National Archives at Kew and Southampton Record Office
Various contemporay newspaper reports

Web-Resources consulted include:
Southern E-group pages at www.semgonline.com
Wikipedia at www.wikipedia.com

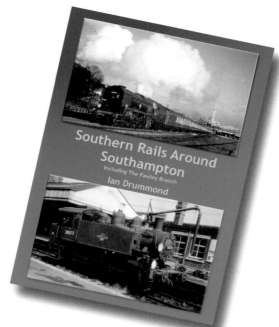
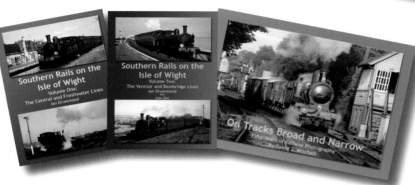
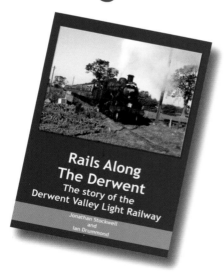